With
Every
Breath
I Take

With Every Breath I Take

One person's extraordinary
journey to a healthy life,
and how you can share in it.

GARY McPHERSON

Copyright © 2000 by Gary McPherson
Printed in Canada
First printed in 2000 5 4 3 2 1

Canadian Cataloguing in Publication Data
McPherson, Gary, 1946–
    With every breath I take

ISBN No. (0-9686724-0-X)

    1. McPherson, Gary, 1946- –Health. 2. Self-care, Health. I. Title.
RA776.95.M36 2000   613   C00-910205-1

Published and distributed by
    Double M Brokerage Ltd.
    14888 - 41st Avenue
    Edmonton, Alberta, Canada T6H 5N7

www.garymcpherson.com

Edited by Carol Berger.
Design and layout by Carol Dragich.
Cover photograph by Robert Chelmick.
Printing by Quality Color Press Inc.

For Clayton May—my friend, mentor, and confidante. He will forever live in my heart and be a part of me.

Contents

Acknowledgments

"I thank God for my handicaps, for through them, I have found myself, my work and my God."

—Helen Keller

This quote by Helen Keller expresses how I feel about my life. I have so much to be thankful for and so many people to thank. When a person becomes dependent on others for most daily living requirements, he or she soon realizes how interdependent the world really is. Without this support I would not have been able to accomplish, share, enjoy, contribute, grow and love to the degree that I have.

I want to thank and acknowledge my mother, Dorothy, who has always been there for me, from the day I was born to the moment I completed this book. She is not only a mom, resource and secretary, but a source of inspiration and a friend.

I have many wonderful friends all over this world and my best friend is my partner Valerie, who has provided us with two beautiful children, Keiko and Jamie. These three are the primary reason that I find myself in better health than ever before in my life. I am truly grateful.

To everyone else who has played a role in my development in any way, shape or form, I am forever indebted and thankful for your kindness and support. This includes my two deceased fathers, David Wilcox and Rod McPherson, my sisters and brothers, Joanne, Scott (deceased), Kim, Ross and Rody.

I was fortunate to have had so many wonderful and dedicated professionals, staff and volunteers from so many different countries and cultures take care of my needs. This gave me an appreciation that few in this world have an opportunity to experience.

I am only sorry that many roommates and friends who were so important to me are not here in person to share this moment of triumph to which we all contributed. Their memory, influence and mentoring will always be a part of my very being. In particular I wish to acknowledge my dear friend who was so special to me and to whom I dedicate this book, Clayton May. Before he met an unfortunate end in the intensive care unit of the University of Alberta Hospital under questionable circumstances, he was responsible for me getting together with my wife, Valerie.

A project like this doesn't come together without a little good fortune and the help of others. It has often been said that one person's misfortune can be another person's opportunity. This was the case for me. I fortunately became reconnected with Cassandra Strumecki, a friend of mine from many years ago, when I found out that she was going through a life-altering experience with breast cancer. She offered to assist me in finishing this book, for which I am truly grateful. It was through her health challenges that we were reconnected. Thank you Cassandra for your friendship, for sharing your skills and talents and, above all, for being you.

Many other people have contributed in some way to shaping this final product. This includes my mother and Cynthia Peterson, who assisted me with some of the grammatical challenges. In addition, Tim Mallandaine and Abraham Liron made a significant contribution in the final stages of this literary effort. Thank you all.

Finally, I take this opportunity to thank my good friend Dr. R. D. (Bob) Steadward, whom my son Jamie Robert was named after, for introducing me through the foreword. Bob is the founding president of the International Paralympic Committee, the international governing body for the Paralympics which, in structure, is the parallel to the International Olympic Committee. In number of participants, the Paralympics is the second largest international sporting event in the world next to the Olympics. Bob is a world leader on several fronts and I am honoured to count him amongst my closest friends. He has taught me so much and I love him dearly.

I truly have been blessed in my lifetime and I wouldn't trade my experiences, friendships, relationships and life for anything.

A special thanks to Carol Berger for her editing capabilities, to Carol Dragich for contributing her graphic and layout talents, Bob Chelmick for his photography and Glenn Rollans for his guidance and encouragement.

Foreword

I have the honour and privilege to present my very close friend and colleague, Dr. Gary William Wilcox McPherson, adjunct professor, community volunteer, provincial administrator and a crusader for the rights and betterment of people with disabilities throughout the world.

When I first met Gary in 1968 he was an amateur ham radio operator. With his assistance we organized the first Canadian wheelchair games. By this time he had already spent thirteen years living in the University Hospital, been involved in several varied activities and had created a partnership in a computer software company with his fellow roommates. Soon thereafter he began to take a leading role in developing sport for athletes with a disability in Edmonton, in Alberta and in Canada.

Gary has an adjunct professorship within the Faculty of Physical Education and Recreation at the University of Alberta. Through the wisdom of his teaching he has been instrumental in fostering initiatives in the area of adapted physical activity. He was selected as a participant in the 1991 Governor General's Canadian Study Conference, a project designed to develop unity and understanding among Canadians.

He has received the highest honours possible in wheelchair sports, the Robert Jackson Award and the Robert Fertile Memorial Award. He has been inducted into both the Edmonton and Alberta Sport Halls of Fame. He was also awarded the King Clancy and the Donald King Memorial National Awards for outstanding contribution to amateur sports in Canada. He was a finalist for the Air Canada Amateur Sports Executive of the Year Award and received the Canadian Occupational and Physical Therapy Association Award for outstanding contribution to the field of rehabilitation. All this in addition to numerous other awards for his outstanding contributions to the community.

Gary's work has gone from Project Hawaii, when he organized a trip to Hawaii for people with polio living in the Aberhart Hospital, to leading provocative and controversial discussions in the areas of equality and equity. Through modelling, informing and cajoling, Gary has pushed the University of Alberta and many communities into recognizing and understanding the needs and desires of persons with disabilities.

Although he lived in an institutional environment for thirty-four years, his ideals and visions relate to each one of us–regardless of our status. He is truly remarkable.

Gary exemplifies the very finest qualities in a human being. He has concern, commitment, enthusiasm, initiative, compassion, pride and integrity. He is a pioneer, a humanitarian, an inspiration of innovative processes and a mentor to everyone who ever thought that they were prevented from following their dreams.

As Dr. Martha Piper, the president of the University of British Columbia, has so aptly said: "To impart facts is simple, to impart knowledge is more difficult, but to impart understanding is truly a gift."

Our community is a much richer environment because of Gary's gift.

Dr. R. D. (Bob) Steadward

Preface

A couple of times a year I and my family visit Katie, my mother-in-law, in Raymond, Alberta. The journey from Edmonton to Raymond takes about five and a half hours each way, covering a total distance of about 1,100 kilometres. Raymond is a quiet Mormon town located about seventeen kilometres south of Lethbridge and has a population of two thousand people. For some unknown reason, my mind becomes more creative when I am sitting at the kitchen table in Katie's house. I somehow feel more inspired when I am there.

It was on one of those visits that the seeds of this book took root. I was reading the *Lethbridge Herald* and came across an article on a young woman in Toronto who was struggling with some sort of respiratory condition. I remember thinking that I would like to have a conversation with her because I was convinced that I had experience that could help her work through some of her respiratory difficulties. I asked myself, "How could I speak to her in the most effective way, without imposing myself?" That is when I knew that I had to write a book. Although I initially planned to write something more focused on respiratory conditions and what could be done to work through some of those challenges, I wound up with a different book than the one I originally planned! This book is the result of the journey from that first idea to completion of the final chapter.

The environment that I grew up in gave me a unique education that will probably never be duplicated again. Because of this, I felt and still feel an obligation to share my life's lessons with those who supported me through it all, through thick and thin. And those who gave that support were, first of all, the taxpayers of Alberta and Canada. Along with them were my family, friends, nursing and medical staff, roommates, volunteers and even those people that I didn't always get along with!

Not only was my education unusual, but my experience working with government showed me that there were major difficulties and challenges related to the health of Canadians which called for help. Like most males, I have an ego and believe that I can offer somewhat of a solution, or at least offer some useful input! Regardless, it is my opinion that health care is a black hole when it comes to financial resources. Because it is a black hole, we will never be able to satisfy its financial appetite.

This book is an attempt to share my personal philosophy as it relates to a healthy lifestyle. The suggestions I offer, the solutions and tips, were in most cases ones that I personally tested. Just so you know, there is nothing very revolutionary or new in this book. But there is some very useful information that has been brought together through a lived experience.

I took this approach because I wanted to demonstrate that each one of us must, and can, do our part to ease the burden on our overworked, questionably organized and demoralized health care systems. If we don't, we are headed for a financial free-fall, not to mention a never-ending series of illnesses which are brought on by a variety of factors. This financial free-fall will be fuelled by economic self-interest, and these interests are virtually unstoppable. The only antidote is to take personal responsibility. This means we each must do our part to take care of the health of ourselves, our neighbours and our communities. We have no choice but to do so.

One of the distressing things in this whole health care debate is the vested interests of certain businesses, governments and professionals who rely on the system for profits and livelihood. Often, these financial interests are not in our–the public's–best interests. This perspective is seldom questioned or challenged because of both the respect and naiveté of the general public.

I don't profess to know it all, but I am one of the few people in this country who has had an opportunity to experience most elements of the health care system. Hopefully, my experience, as told in this book, will be useful to you.

Our future personal understanding of health is likely to become even more clouded and, therefore, still more difficult for the average person to comprehend. Every day we are fed conflicting health messages through the various modes of electronic communication, ranging from newspaper articles to information on the Internet (which, incidentally, is often a primary source for the media). Also, more and more research is being funded by private interests and this can, and does, affect the way research results are used. Even though scientific research is an imperfect art, we sometimes embrace the results we want to hear without looking deeper. This is understandable. We are all inclined to want a quick result, the magic bullet that is somehow promised through the marvels of science and technology.

This desire for a magic bullet for whatever illness or disease that man or God creates is magnified through the ongoing human genome project that is being financed by certain federal governments and the pharmaceutical industry. The human genome project is ahead of schedule and promises to deliver a genetic map of our DNA makeup. Armed with this information we can look towards a future that promises to deliver more drugs, medications, gene therapies and medical interventions for whatever condition one might have in his or her lifetime. These conditions could range from the period of pre-conception and into the throes of old age. This is all taking place at a time when the medical establishment is struggling to cope with new strains of superbugs that are resistant to manufactured antibiotics. Our current approach to health and health care assures that there will be still more of these superbugs! We will surrender even more control over our well-being to the medical and pharmaceutical industry.

I fear that all of this means that we are actually moving further away from health and further and further away from recognizing that good health is mostly the result of good habits! Habits are learned through a variety of teachings and instilled through practice, repetition and some self-discipline.

My experience tells me that maintaining personal health requires a daily commitment to a healthy lifestyle. Health is mostly about habit. It is up to each one of us to instil the necessary habits that contribute to healthy living and a more rewarding life.

Introduction

Significant changes are occurring in the health care system in Canada and around the world. The government tells us that it must cut its spending on the health care system. Hospitals and physicians tell us that our systems need more money if our health is not to be compromised. What should we believe?

In my view the health care systems, as currently organized, have an insatiable appetite for dollars and, therefore, it will never be possible to provide what could be termed "sufficient" funds. The reason is because the primary, and almost single focus, is on illness and disease. Though we are lucky to have such a health care system when we need it, we also need a system that will maintain and improve our health.

We can't expect the health care system to furnish us with good health. We have to rely on ourselves and take responsibility for nurturing our own health. To do this, we need knowledge, skills and motivation.

People have been bombarded with conflicting messages and bits of information from many directions, including propaganda from those with vested interests. Every day we can read about a new study, a new syndrome, a newly discovered genetic defect or some other information which tells us to do the opposite of what we were doing the day before. What is a person to do?

What I have to say is not very revolutionary. What I am doing is sharing some of the lessons I learned while growing up in the medical care environment and, more importantly, what I have learned away from the medical care system. I believe it is the latter that will help the reader as we move forward into the twenty-first century.

If this book does nothing more than get people talking and thinking in a new direction—a direction which entails self-responsibility and looking out for the best interests of one another—then it will have been worth it. If we don't take control and provide the required antidote for ourselves and for one another, we will become the accomplices of illness and disease.

I hope that when you have finished reading this book you will have found some answers. I also hope that you can use one or more of my suggestions to improve your health and maybe even your life. There are many messages contained herein and perhaps there will be one for you.

The Beginning of My Journey

GROWING UP

I grew up in the largest active treatment hospital in Alberta. The University of Alberta Hospital, while my home, was also one of the largest such facilities in all of Canada. For many of my years there, I was the youngest patient on the polio ward. This meant that many people took an interest in my well-being. Children who are disabled, or in dire circumstances, often get to our heartstrings. I was both.

Because I was too busy fighting for the next breath of air and surviving from one medical crisis to the next, I had neither the time nor the inclination to dwell on what I couldn't do. I think I probably experienced almost every major intrusive intervention that was possible. This was because of my need to be ventilated and the requirement for a tracheotomy to help clear my airway. I faced many problems with this aspect of my care. Looking back, I survived both because of, and in spite of, these interventions which were for the most part extremely uncomfortable.

The first challenge was one of survival. Thanks to the heroic efforts of many medical professionals and caregivers, supported by the intestinal

I

fortitude of others who were resident on the polio ward, many of us did survive and become contributors to society.

The second challenge was dealing emotionally with the many medical crises that people who became my family had to deal with. Not only were the immediate challenges an issue, but death would often intrude and eliminate one of us, leaving behind many hard-to-handle emotional responses.

I didn't realize then that what we think about our health and circumstance will often affect the eventual outcome. Upon reflection, I am sure that certain health or lack-of-health situations that occurred could have been reversed, or prevented, with what we know today about approaches to care that involve not only the body but also the mind and the soul. These approaches could have complemented the efforts of the professionals.

Death was everpresent and often occupied my thoughts. It seemed that some people whom I perceived as being healthier than me, or more deserving, were dying. What did that mean for me? Who would be next? If one wants to move forward in life, these are not good thoughts to have on a regular basis.

This often involved people who had become closer to me, in certain ways, than my immediate family. This was because we often had many of the same challenges and were a great source of support to one another. There was a love and personal bond between us that is difficult for me to describe.

THINKING I WAS UNHEALTHY

It is not too difficult to figure out that illness, disease and poor health permeated my life from a very early age. In addition, hospitals and in particular intensive care areas are rife with various difficult-to-manage or hard-to-kill bugs. This further complicated our lives.

I was in Grade 5 when I got polio. For the first several months following the onset, school was not a priority. After my condition had stabilized, school became a way to occupy free time. School consisted of a combination of classroom instruction involving multiple grades and correspondence lessons from the Correspondence School Branch.

Again, the reality of poor health was reinforced through my exposure in the classroom. The classroom sessions were conducted on the children's ward and it was virtually the only time that I interacted with other children. It was during such a session that I first witnessed an epileptic seizure and met someone with leukemia. Neither one of these exposures was very encouraging or reassuring.

Because I was physically unable to write, volunteers became a very important part of my educational support structure. Their willingness, time and generosity would play a significant role in shaping my future.

I remember working with one of these volunteer ladies, answering questions via correspondence. The subject was health and most of the questions regarding my personal health status were very difficult for me to answer. The reason they were difficult was because I was confused and didn't know how to accurately assess my condition or situation.

I didn't know how to answer the simple question: What is the state of your health? There were three or four choices, such as poor, fair, good, excellent. I was confused because I felt good, although I was often battling a respiratory condition that would involve congestion of some sort. This was not even considering my need to use a ventilator for more than twenty hours a day and the fact that I was significantly paralyzed with quadriplegia. For most people, the answers to the questions would have been obvious. For me, however, the ventilator had become a friend and quadriplegia was now a part of my physical identity. I no longer thought of either of them as being a negative in my life.

I believe that because I was young when I got polio it was easier on me than on most of the adults who were my roommates. I was both young and naive, which worked to my advantage. When you don't know better, it is easier to persist. And, because of this, fewer artificial barriers are created to prevent one from moving forward in a positive manner. This certainly was the case for me. It was this naiveté that made the simple questions about my health so difficult to answer.

I also remember living my earlier life in five-year increments. The reason for this was because the life expectancy for people who had a severe respiratory condition combined with a physical disability was not very long. I got the impression from somewhere (maybe it was just the environment I lived in), that five years of life was all that could be hoped for. I was surprised to find myself alive at fourteen years of age, and again at nineteen.

It was because of this thinking around life expectancy that I thought school was really a waste of time. Before getting polio I was an excellent student and extremely competitive. I found this not to be the case with Correspondence School. It was difficult to get motivated, particularly if I wasn't going to live an adult life. In spite of this attitude towards my schoolwork, I was very active through socialization, playing games, attending sporting events and concerts, and just doing things that were of interest to me. It was this general activity which became the foundation upon which I built my life.

A MAJOR REVELATION

Something that is not very well understood by the general public, and to some degree by those in the medical and other professions, is sexuality and people with disabilities. This book gives me an opportunity to share with you that I, along with my disabled brethren, are sexual beings with capabilities, feelings and emotions that are considered normal, whatever normal is. Some medical conditions can make it difficult for normal reproduction to take place, but in my experience this is more the exception than the rule. Fortunately, I am one of those individuals who retained all of my sexual capabilities, as polio does not affect sexual function. At this point, I want to make it very clear that in most cases, paralysis and sexual dysfunction are not necessarily synonymous and that paralysis does not affect the need for intimacy. Seldom does it inhibit sexual desire. In other words, a person with a disability is a human being with sexual desires.

The fact that I have been able to regain and to retain my health has allowed me to make the commitment to marriage and to have children, just as most people can do. I didn't always know or realize that I had both the capacity and capabilities to marry and reproduce because this was never taught to me, or expected of me, by those on whom I was dependent. Therefore, regarding sexuality, no one should feel badly about their lack of knowledge and understanding towards people who have a physical disability. In order to truly understand that my desires and capability were no different from those of most people, I took courses and learned through personal experience. Our systems and culture somehow perpetuate the myth that disabled individuals are less able and less relevant. In my opinion and experience, this is untrue.

I lived in the University Hospital and the Aberhart Centre for thirty-four years. I probably could have moved out earlier with proper community support, such as home care, to address my personal and daily requirements. But until I became involved with Valerie, I didn't have a big enough reason to move into the community, to leave the protective institutional environment that I called home. It was when we decided to have children that I decided to marry Valerie. It was only then that I had a big enough reason to leave the confines of my secure institutional home.

Another major hurdle for me, both in psychological and practical terms, was leaving the Aberhart. As soon as I moved out of the Aberhart and into the community, everything that I had taken for granted—accommodation, meals, bathing, getting up, going to bed, the expense of additional amenities—now became my personal responsibility. This meant that I had to not only organize this aspect of my life, but also pay for most, if not all, of it. Make no mistake, this was a huge psychological barrier and a major disincentive for me to overcome.

A permanent relationship and marriage were not something that I expected in my life, even though I often longed for companionship that would include a physical relationship. Looking back, I probably missed one or more opportunities to establish a long-term relationship. This was because of my institutional inhibitions, all contained within my institutional mindset. Even though I have been able to transcend the institutional mould, I may still retain some institutional scars and markings that are reflected in my current thoughts and actions.

ACTIVITY AND HEALTH

I didn't realize it at the time, but volunteerism not only changed my life, it changed my health. I learned that in order to be active and do the various things that I enjoyed, I would have to take care of my health in ways that I had never before thought of.

There were several significant milestones or points of change in my life. One of the biggest was when I joined the Junior Chamber of Commerce, today known as the Jaycees. I immersed myself in all aspects of the Edmonton Jaycees and took every personal development course offered, applying the lessons learned through the various internal committees. This proved to be an invaluable training ground for my life. First of all, I proved to myself that I could compete in the real world outside the University Hospital. I was respected and valued by my fellow Jaycee members, and I received numerous awards and recognition within the organization for outstanding contributions.

The various awards were initially very important to me because I was still developing my self-esteem. The biggest and most satisfying recognition was when I ran in the democratic, political-style elections that were held on an annual basis. I was initially elected as a director and later to the executive.

After being involved up to my neck in Jaycees for three and a half years, I had to make a major decision: Should I run for president of the organization? During my membership, the organization's presidents were outstanding and probably overly committed, to the point that the position's responsibilities impinged on family life.

This raised the question: Could I withstand the physical demand on my body and how would it affect my health?

There was no longer any doubt in my mind that I could responsibly and effectively carry out the duties as president, but health remained a big question mark in my mind. Even though all of the Jaycee meetings (dinner and board) were held in totally inaccessible venues, this had not deterred my involvement in any way.

I must confess that I came close to needing to change my pants on several occasions while being carried up and down the steps that led to the Captain's Cabin for dinner gatherings, and the Jaycee office where the board meetings were held. Having to deal with the personal anxiety created by the generosity of a variety of uneducated help in the form of my willing Jaycee compatriots, combined with the twenty-six steps that were a part of both venues, also proved invaluable in helping me overcoming other obstacles in life.

Due to health factors and physical access barriers, I made the decision to leave Jaycees. I believed that the presidency was beyond me. I had not yet realized that I could affect change in both areas. Little did I know that both would become a part of my life's work.

I acquired many important skills and developed my organizational and administrative talents, as well as making many lifelong friendships during my tenure with the Jaycees. The most important skill that I developed was public speaking. Like most people, I was very afraid of getting in front of people and exposing my limited knowledge, disability and lack of confidence. Fortunately, through external support, and knowing that I had to do it, I was able to overcome my inhibitions.

I overcame my anxieties by taking the various speaking and parliamentary procedure courses offered, and complemented the classroom sessions by teaching the effective speaking course to student nurses at the Royal Alexandra Hospital. This arrangement, whereby Jaycees taught student nurses, was a mutual relationship that had been established before I joined the organization. I also entered the area speaking competition for the Jaycees and placed second to a chap who went on to win the national competition. This was great for my confidence.

Besides overcoming my inhibitions and anxieties, I had the challenge of my voluntary breathing requirements due to my respiratory paralysis. Teaching speaking classes and competing improved my skills and further strengthened the personal foundation that I was developing. Speaking and parliamentary procedure would become cornerstones of my strengths as I journeyed through my voluntary and professional career.

HEALTH BECOMES A PRIORITY

It seems that everything happens for a reason and a purpose. If we look for the lessons, it usually serves us, even if we don't realize it at the time. The decision I arrived at, to leave the Jaycees because of concern about my personal stamina and overall health, was the encouragement I needed to make health a major priority in my life. Without good health I would be extremely limited.

I must confess that not believing I could affect and control my health, to a large degree, prevented me from pursuing a higher education, led to the postponement of marriage opportunities and, if only in a subtle way, affected every decision I made. It was time for me to take control, inch by inch, in an incremental though unplanned fashion.

It began with a fundraising project that we conducted for the Paralympic Sports Association, the organization that I became president of when I left the Jaycees. The project was a wheel-a-thon. We ran the project at a local shopping centre using their parking lot. The main objective was to raise as much money as possible through individual sponsorships and donations.

Up until this time I had always viewed physical activity and exercise as something that applied to other people and not to me. However, I was the president and, based on my Jaycee experience, realized that I had to lead by example, if at all possible. How could I do this? Once I asked myself the question the answer was presented to me.

After all, I could wheel my wheelchair backwards, even though it was difficult for me to see where I was going. Nevertheless, I could still push my chair. I did this, propelled myself, by using my left leg. There was approximately three weeks remaining before the wheel-a-thon was to take place. This meant that if I trained I might be in shape to wheel a few laps around the parking lot.

I then began a crude training program. Every day my friend Larry Barber took me to push my wheelchair around whatever track we could find that was open and available. I was operating under some additional handicaps, in the form of inappropriate equipment and lack of knowledge about how to train, or even what to do.

I had this Everest & Jennings wheelchair that weighed approximately forty-five pounds. This was okay for pushing on linoleum or cement, but was not very easy on a cinder track. I also didn't have the proper shoes. But that didn't deter me. The shoes I wore during those days were Hush Puppies because I found the soles useful for getting traction on tile and linoleum floors. Again, they were not ideal for pushing on a cinder track.

There is no question that I developed a very strong quadricep muscle in my left leg. I also developed calluses on my foot from pushing my chair. I almost killed myself when I wouldn't quit training even though, at times, I would see stars. This was because I was not getting enough air. I was forgetting to breathe deeply and often. With my involuntary breathing muscles paralyzed, I was unable to get adequate ventilation. During training, I was overworking those voluntary muscles that were compensating for the paralyzed ones. Eventually, I learned that regular exercise improved my breathing capability.

My objective was to wheel four times around the shopping centre parking lot. Based on doing only four laps, I hustled my sponsorships at the University Hospital. I did, however, let the would-be donors know that I might go further if I felt strong enough. Many of my donors pledged one dollar per lap, thinking that anything less than one dollar would be chintzy. What neither I nor they suspected then, was that I would wind up doing twenty laps and ultimately raise eleven hundred dollars out of a total fundraising aggregate of $7,700.

The important lesson here was not that I did twenty laps or that I raised any amount of money, but rather that I proved that I could, and should, exercise on a regular basis. It was at this point in my life that exercise became a regular part of my routine. That was in 1972.

Understanding
the Health
Culture

When I first contracted polio the people who looked after me were literally just out of school, or in fact may have not finished school. They were working in an environment where people were very ill and where many died. Today some of those same people are working in highly specialized medical environments with no formal academic medical training. What they do have is a medical background that encompasses a practical and human experience. In my view they were, and are, among the best of caregivers. In those days they were referred to as ward aids and orderlies.

During my hospital years, the medical hierarchy had doctors at the top, BScNs next, followed by RNs, RNAs (today's LPNs), registered orderlies, orderlies, aides and cleaning staff. Yet, in my experience, their bedside qualities of patient care were often directly opposite in relation to hierarchy. The creation of this hierarchy within the health care delivery system was probably done to create status and prestige and provided a way to clearly delineate the lines of authority, responsibility and financial compensation.

When I first went home to spend an afternoon with my family, my mother was regularly required to suction me through my tracheotomy. This is a procedure that was taught to her by aides or orderlies who

9

worked with me in the acute stages of my rehabilitation. Some fifteen to twenty years later, rules and regulations prevented the less educated in the hierarchy of nursing from performing the same suctioning procedures as they had before. Eventually, we were able to change this on our hospital ward, but it still held true for the rest of the hospital.

At the time, I recall that family, friends and volunteers were also very involved in supplementing nursing care, which made life a whole lot more enjoyable under some very difficult circumstances where people were acutely ill.

Of course, in the minds of those who enforced the rules, such help could also create problems. It could supposedly interfere with what was termed "the routine," like visiting hours, meal times and bath times. It seemed to me that most of the rules were created for the convenience of the staff rather than the patients. Little did I know that I would spend most of my life working to break such rules and reshape hospital policy. This all began as the polio ward, which became more chronic-care and long-term in nature, evolved within the setting of one of the largest acute care hospitals in Canada.

Experiencing these types of situations, growing up and living in an institutional environment with all of its human dynamics, taught me a great deal about people, motivation and what a person has to do to bring people together for a common purpose. I also learned a great deal about politics in the organizational sense.

One of the major changes that occurred in nursing was the introduction of respiratory therapy to the University Hospital. Respiratory therapy eventually became an integral part of the respiratory polio ward where I lived. The polio epidemic, with its acute respiratory needs, laid the groundwork for intensive care units (ICUs) as we know them today. It was a most interesting environment to grow up in. It is worth noting that there were no respiratory therapists when the polio epidemic took place.

Even though we have reached the year 2000, in some ways we seem to be going back to where we were forty years ago. The complicating factor in the progress of health care is the advent of technology and the de-institutionalization of patient care. Evolving medical technology, in some cases, requires more knowledge than what was needed in the 1950s. It also requires bio-technical or bio-medical skills. Unfortunately, the de-institutionalization of patient care will lower wages because you don't necessarily need to have a university education to give quality care which involves warmth, love, empathy and the ability to get along with people. All of these ingredients are extremely important for people who are recovering or living with chronic conditions.

There may, in fact, need to be a pecking order within the health care system and there are some wonderful, well-educated and bright nurses who have BScN degrees. I know because one married me or, I could say, I married her. The fact that she married me doesn't necessarily make her bright but, I tell you, she makes me look pretty good. People, being who they are and the fact that most of them are not knowledgeable about disabled people and their capabilities, sometimes raise questions about her judgment but not mine!

I am reminded of the story of when Val and I bought our first home, a condominium on Whyte Avenue about five blocks from the Aberhart Centre. It turned out that our immediate next door neighbour, Mrs. Thompson, had been a nurse on the University Hospital polio ward back in the early 1960s. At this point I should tell you that there was always plenty of gossip on our ward, and probably on all wards. In fact—you can ask virtually anybody who attended them—the "reports" or "conferencing" that took place at shift change were more like gossip sessions than an actual exchange of pertinent medical information. It was difficult to develop a social life in this environment, unless you had thick skin and were oblivious to what people thought or said.

Getting back to Mrs. Thompson, she had a friend on the fourth floor in the same condo complex and, unbeknownst to her, this person was also a friend of my wife. Mrs. Thompson told this mutual friend that her new neighbour was going to be one of her ex-patients and that he had married and was moving out of the Aberhart. She added that it must have been some stupid nurse! We eventually heard about this and, needless to say, we had a good chuckle. In terms of gossip, she hadn't missed a beat and it brought back a flood of memories, which contained some wonderful times.

When I lived in the hospital I learned a great deal about illness, disease and trauma. Conversely, when I got married and moved out of the hospital my education about health really began. This education led me to adopt new beliefs and to further change my lifestyle. My research introduced me to people, places and perspectives that challenged many of my old beliefs and other aspects of what I had learned during my thirty-four years in a hospital environment. After reading, discussing, reflecting and experimenting, I now have a totally different mindset from the one I had when I left the Aberhart Centre in 1989.

In the next few chapters I will attempt to share some of the lessons that I have learned through observation and personal life experiences. For some of you, the things I say will be disturbing and no doubt challenge your current beliefs about medical care and personal health. For others, it will either corroborate or provide a missing element in your personal journey to improved health. In the process I also hope to convince you of why we must, and how we can, take control of our personal health and well-being. I only ask that you read with an open mind, and that you find it within yourself to continue your own research with a view to taking control of your health.

THE MARRIAGE OF SCIENCE AND MEDICINE

"We should be on our guard not to overestimate science and scientific methods when it is a question of human problems; and we should not assume that experts are the only ones who have a right to express themselves on questions affecting the organization of society."

—Albert Einstein

It is useful and instructive to have a basic understanding of the interdependent relationship and importance of science to Western medicine. This will assist us in understanding how doctors have become so powerful and authoritative in our current culture.

In the early 1900s, alternative practitioners outnumbered what we now call Western medicine practitioners by about two to one. This all changed as the number of Western practitioners increased and the power base changed. It culminated with the establishment of rules, regulations and codes that were adopted to regulate all medical practitioners. These rules were contained in the historic Flexner Report. Dr. Guylaine Lanctot, in her book titled *The Medical Mafia*, makes the point that the adoption of the Flexner Report was the beginning of the end for alternative practitioners in the Western hemisphere. It was this report, and the rules and regulations contained therein, that shaped the teachings in North American medical schools. With the adoption of these new rules, alternative practitioners were seriously limited.

A doctor who practised allopathic medicine in earlier times really did not have any solid scientific basis on which to validate his practice and treatments. In other words, he relied on instinct, experience, known information and, basically, common sense. Because there didn't seem to be any scientific validity to the practice of Western medicine, it was necessary to introduce science through various research approaches. It was this marriage of scientific research and medical practice that formed the foundation of the current health system in most developed countries.

In a respected medically related publication entitled *The Pharos,* John Wesley Boyd explained how medicine has depicted science as being both objective and dispassionate. It is through this perception of being both objective and dispassionate that medicine uses science as a screen, or filter, for validation. Consequently, this view of medicine and science has established an air of credibility and authority that medicine didn't have a century ago.

Mr. Boyd concluded his article by observing that science obviously plays a significant role in the credibility of medicine and thus is paraded as being essential to the efficacy of new therapies and health technology. Understandably, therefore, the last thing that medicine wants is for science to appear less objective. Without the authority guaranteed it by its affiliation with science, medicine would run the risk of returning to the days when all that it had to offer was the personal authority of (some of) its practitioners.

The worldwide medical culture that persists today, and which is now in financial difficulty, was entrenched by the United Nations' 1977 adoption of the Flexner Report through the passage of the Alma-Ata Declaration. This gave unparalleled powers to the World Health Organization (WHO), which is in effect the Surgeon General for the UN.

The late popular Nobel Laureate physicist Richard Feynman once commented:

> When a scientist doesn't know the answer to a problem, he is ignorant. When he has a hunch as to what the result is, he is uncertain. And when he is pretty darn sure of what the result is going to be, he is still in some doubt. Scientific knowledge is a body of statements of varying degrees of certainty—some mostly unsure, some nearly sure, but none absolutely certain.

Considering that science is often surrounded by uncertainty and that there is an inextricable human element involved, doesn't it suggest that our unquestionable faith in medicine and its relationship with science might be misplaced? It is my personal view that science and curative research is at its best suspect and, at its worst, faulty.

In one of her speeches to a graduating medical class, Dr. Marlys Witte shared the fact that she had started a curriculum in 1985 on "medical ignorance, failure, and chaos" in response to growing criticisms of medical education. Dr. Witte explained that the intent of the course was to address the shortcomings and limits of medicine.

In that same speech Dr. Witte commented that many high-profile surgeries, including transplants, which are heralded as medical "triumphs" are not cures but rather tacit acknowledgment of a profound ignorance of the body's wayward biochemistry and physiology. It is now possible to better understand how we have come to blindly put our faith in physicians. By placing our faith in physicians to the degree that we have, we have at the same time, unknowingly legitimized science, even when it deserves to be questioned and held in doubt. This may explain why the truth moves: a treatment or procedure that is used today may have been ridiculed the day before, or even held in contempt.

To illustrate why we can no longer blindly have faith in the advice of our physicians, I make reference to a speech that was given in Toronto, Canada, by Dr. Susan Love, the renowned breast surgeon. She emphasized that we must move beyond early detection to the prevention of such illnesses as breast cancer. She stated: "We all have to be our own advocate. You can't trust the medical profession. If you see 160 patients a week, you don't have time to read articles. You know where most doctors get their information? From drug salesmen."

Dr. Love further emphasized that the most important thing we can do for women's health is to increase the time devoted to exercise for girls in high school and encourage a diet high in fruits and vegetables.

Hopefully, this information will help us understand why we as individuals need to become more involved and better informed about health options, for our own interests and those of our families.

WHAT DRIVES MEDICAL CARE COSTS?

There are many factors that contribute to the exorbitant cost of medical care and all that it entails. One of the biggest contributors is society's philosophical and cultural approach to the field of health care.

I believe that our philosophy and beliefs, whether personal or collective, are expressed in the words, phrases and the labels that we use in articulating our thoughts. In the field of medicine this expression of our philosophy is of paramount importance. According to William S. Burroughs, "Language is a virus." Our current approach to the field of medicine needs a rethink. Maybe we should begin with how we describe what we are doing. In our collectives, what choices do we make when we use different words, phrases and labels?

The disease, or medical model, permeates all aspects of society. It has shaped the way we label social problems before attempting to fix or cure them. On the surface, this medicalization of social problems may seem to have advantages. But it also means labelling people and their conditions.

The downside for all concerned is that, for the most part, labels are damaging and destructive for the individual who has been labelled, and who must then live with the label.

The moment a person and his or her support network, or society, buys into the label, many things happen. The most important thing that happens is the way the label shapes our beliefs, individually and collectively. The beliefs shape our personal and societal values and can be very difficult to change, even when new and credible information is presented. I make these statements believing, for the most part, that the restoration of social, psychological and vocational functioning are much more important than the physical or curative aspects that drive current medical research.

Our obsession with looking at illness and disease as an enemy to be annihilated has shaped a philosophy which says we must rid ourselves of the enemy at all costs. Now these costs are becoming prohibitive for all societies and their citizens. By putting almost unlimited resources into technology, pharmaceuticals, research and personnel in order to vanquish the enemy, we have created an untenable financial position for ourselves. When you combine this military approach with market forces, which means profits before people, the costs become exponential and out of control. We must take control and do what is best for people, their families and their communities.

PROFITS, PEOPLE, PHARMACEUTICALS AND PROFESSIONALS

When I was extensively involved in the administration of wheelchair sports, I sometimes joked that in order to recruit new wheelchair athletes we should get involved in the promotion of motorcycle sales and let the polio virus out of the laboratory. This would have assisted in the recruitment of new athletes but, at the same time, would have been both ethically and morally wrong. This was in reference to the fact that most wheelchair athletes in the early development of wheelchair sports were either paralyzed with a spinal cord injury or paralyzed to some degree by polio. This would have solved our recruitment problems, but it certainly wouldn't have been in the best interests of individuals, families and their communities.

As we move forward into the twenty-first century, we must address our health care questions to the "people model," with less emphasis on profits. If we do not do this, we will not be able to sustain our individual and collective health. My reasoning has more to do with what I think is right, and less to do with any personal political ideology. In December

1996 the Pope said, "It is necessary and urgent that nations begin to follow economic and nutritional policies founded not only on profit, but on solidarity." I strongly believe that these words from Pope John Paul are meant for all of us and not just for members of the Roman Catholic and Orthodox churches.

More often than not, there is an inherent conflict between what is expedient and what is right. It will take considerable effort, cooperation and a sincere interest, individually, collectively and globally, to begin to stem the tide of consumerism and multinational interests which are in conflict with what is best for people and their communities.

There are some things in life that we don't question. We seem to accept them as gospel. One such area, at least up until recently, has been health care (medical care) and the role and responsibility of major players in the medical care system. We have given doctors supreme power and authority to make decisions on our behalf. This authority and our willingness to place the medical profession on a pedestal has coloured our thinking and distracted us from asking more in-depth questions about what is in the best interest of people.

Our naiveté has allowed the major players and, in particular, the pharmaceutical industry to grow exponentially. This growth has been with almost no involvement, direction or scrutiny by the lay public. Consequently, the pharmaceutical industry now virtually controls all curative research. Also, the pharmaceutical industry usually determines what research takes place through both its financial clout and political influence. More often than not, the curative research that takes place in labs throughout the world is controlled by a handful of very powerful interests.

These interests prey on the public's fears of becoming incapacitated through illness, disease and disability. They continue on the basis that there is a magic cure for virtually every ill that exists or will exist. We accept this premise without question, in the hope that it is true. Generally speaking, that is what drives the human genome project and genetic research.

My personal experience leads me to estimate that at least ninety per cent of the curative research never reaches the end user. Nor does it provide benefits. It is this potential end user who is supposedly the reason for the research being done in the first place.

We are spending billions of dollars on research and pharmaceutical products that provide limited, if any, benefit. What is really bothersome about this is that there are many of these same subjects (people) who cannot get home care, barrier free transportation or a variety of technical aids that would allow them to function and contribute to themselves, their families and their communities. We perpetuate the myth that we can fix people when we use this approach.

We have created a financial and economic giant that is pivotal to economies everywhere. An unfortunate aspect of all this is that governments in all parts of the world are reluctant to, or can't, affect change because they rely on the economic spin-off and employment opportunities generated by the pharmaceutical industry. Also, governments are lobbied intensively by powerful individuals seeking tax concessions and legislation and regulations that are beneficial to the industry.

Another dilemma for governments is where do they turn for objective advice as to what is the right or best thing to do, given the significant influence of the pharmaceutical companies and by dependent association, the medical profession? In most cases, this gives the industry an inordinate amount of influence and, for all intents and purposes, makes industry both the adjudicator and the beneficiary.

To take it further, the pharmaceutical industry controls the research journals, decides who sits on peer-adjudicated committees, chooses material to be published and shared at conferences and provides university grants. There is strong evidence to suggest that, in some cases, research results are either manipulated or omitted in order to get favourable results in the testing of new drugs. I know this seems hard to believe but it must be remembered that large entities can often purchase any result they want. The stakes are high and the tentacles of the pharmaceutical industry are everywhere.

In order to make sense of medical reports in the media, you need to know how medical studies are conducted and how even the best ones can go astray.

The accepted methodology and the most reliable results are usually obtained by what is called a randomized, double-blind clinical trial. Patients suffering the same disease are randomly divided into two groups. The patients in one group receive a placebo and those in the other group receive the drug that is being tested. To eliminate possible bias, neither the doctors nor the patients know which group is which, hence the term double-blind. Researchers overseeing the project keep track of who is getting the real treatment.

While this is the standard method for testing new drugs and medical procedures, it has its limitations. Even these measures can't guarantee that a study will be problem-free. Double-blind clinical trials will not predict how to keep people healthy. Researchers are limited in what they can do.

For instance, when doing drug-specific research, it is usually difficult or impossible to take into consideration with any degree of accuracy, lifestyle, diet and environmental factors.

Another factor is, no matter how hard we try, controlled studies are prone to false evidence, simply because there are so many mitigating factors when dealing with human subjects. What takes place in a laboratory with animals will in all probability only give us an idea of what to expect with humans. One of the great difficulties is that humans are not in the same sense, "animals" per se. The human mind and our thought processes have a powerful effect on what takes place within our bodies after we've taken medicine or other substances such as food. This has been proven through the placebo effect.

There are other factors in trying to translate laboratory results into actual human practice that further complicate this fact. The reason is we all think as individuals, with positive and negative impacts on our emotions, feelings and ultimately our health. In our culture, we have blindly accepted much of the information from the pharmaceutical industry and medical profession as gospel. Our confidence in what has been a "given" in our lives is now being challenged. I think that this shaken confidence will lead to improved health because it will force us to be more responsible for ourselves.

Globe and Mail medical reporter Paul Taylor wrote a series of articles on medical research and the pharmaceutical industry. His articles demonstrated the shortcomings of mixing scientific principles with practical application and study. He stated: "Avid readers of medical news should always keep in mind that studies can still be limited by faulty methodology, research bias and the inability of any one study to be all-encompassing."

We, the unsuspecting public, should know that even when studies have been peer reviewed, pharmaceutical companies often hire public relations firms to give their test results the best possible spin. In doing so, they will often line up medical experts for the reporters to interview. It should come as no surprise that these medical experts who are quoted in news stories are often paid consultants to the pharmaceutical companies in question.

The Health Protection Branch of the Department of Health and Welfare Canada and the Food and Drug Administration (FDA) in the United States presumably are there to represent the best interests of the Canadian and US citizenry. Often the decisions that are made by these regulatory bodies seem in contradiction with this principle. In a letter to the editor of a major national magazine, one individual suggested that the Health Protection Branch was an appropriate title because it certainly seemed to protect Canadians from their health. This individual was referring to decisions that appear to be in the best interests of corporations and often to the detriment of the individual consumer.

Similarly, the FDA has often been accused of being in bed with the pharmaceutical industry. The primary reason for these accusations is that the two have been known to exchange highly placed executives who collaborate and then are instrumental in making recommendations and decisions that affect you and me. From an objective perspective this could appear to be incestuous, if not, bordering on the corrupt.

One cannot help but be suspicious when remedies, treatments and a variety of therapies are denied people who are in very difficult circumstances. These same people are then forced to seek help to alleviate their pain and suffering outside North America. For example, treatments such as ozone therapy are commonplace in Germany and are reported to have significant health benefits for patients. Yet ozone therapy is not readily available to Canadians or Americans. When alternative medical practitioners make these treatments available to their patients, they are either threatened or suspended by their regulatory bodies. As a society we need to force this issue.

The advent of food supplements and the evolution of the nutriceutical industry is making the pharmaceutical industry nervous. This is because the pharmaceutical interests might lose some of their markets as the public becomes more knowledgeable. This has resulted in pharmaceutical companies attempting to buy up as many patents as possible where they relate to the research and future development of nutriceuticals.

To indicate how absurd and confused the future might become, we need look no further than the following two examples. In the first case, the US Patent Office revoked a patent granted to researchers from the University of Mississippi. The patent previously gave the university monopoly rights on a turmeric-based process to heal wounds. This decision was precipitated by a spirited and well-documented challenge by the Indian Council for Scientific and Industrial Research.

The Indian agency's argument was simply that turmeric has been used as a healing agent for wounds in India for centuries and is part of existing public knowledge. Therefore, there is nothing new or novel about it that could make it the basis for an exclusive patent.

The second case involves neem, which is a tree that grows all over India and neighbouring Asian countries. For more than two thousand years its twigs and leaves have been used for everything from birth control to pesticides. Yet a corporation has been granted a patent in the US on it as a "new" product. The patent on neem, along with dozens of others from all over the world, have been approved by this same US Patent Office that wisely revoked the turmeric patent.

Bio-diversity and genetic engineering are huge issues. The reason for this is that by altering a single gene of a healing herb a drug manufacturer can claim that it is a "new" product. This makes it eligible to be locked under a patent for a certain number of years.

At stake are billions of dollars. If the public starts switching to natural remedies in a big way, then the drug companies want to be there with their versions first.

I believe this flurry of interest in the nutriceutical industry by the pharmaceutical companies comes with an intent to inhibit and control the development of this young industry. If nutriceuticals could become an industry along with foodaceuticals and food supplements, however, it might be an economic solution for governments and, at the same time, in the best interests of the public. These are tough questions for all of us. Genetic manipulation, with regards to food, is affecting each and every one of us, whether we like it or not.

In my more naive and less skeptical life I was under the impression that all doctors (not just some), and the pharmaceutical companies were in business for more altruistic reasons. Those reasons included wanting to do what is right and best for you and me. Unfortunately, the more I study and learn about the entire medically related industry, the more disillusioned I become with the insidious self-interests that hold an unsuspecting public up for ransom at almost every turn. This is not to discount the fact that there are some wonderful physicians who care deeply about their patients.

In my view, the only challenge to the power and influence of drug companies will come from an enlightened public. This enlightenment is beginning with the search for alternative methods for health and healing, which is becoming more prevalent in our developed world.

It is against this backdrop that I wish to illustrate, through some of my experiences, the importance of taking personal responsibility for our health. Almost every day, we hear about the need to make better use of our tax dollars. This means that we all must look to what we can do to positively impact our health. Ultimately, it is up to you and me!

WHY WE MUST TAKE RESPONSIBILITY

Even though I grew up in the medical care system and owe my life to some heroic interventions by skilled medical personnel, everything I learned about health I learned away from the system that I grew up in. I understand the system which we are trying to change from the inside looking out, as opposed to the outside looking in.

When it comes to health, we are left to fend for ourselves and for our families. But we haven't been taught how to do this. We have grown up in a culture that has promoted a dependency on professionals, drugs, antibiotics and junk food. Unfortunately, this has often been done in the name of profits, power, status, authority and influence, and without regard for the best interests of the masses.

Socioeconomic status has proven to be one of the biggest factors in the health status of various segments of the population, with the lower rung, particularly the impoverished, being most affected. It is this population which accesses the medical care facilities on a regular basis. Its dependency has been assured from very early on. If we really care about people, we must turn this around. If we are to make a difference, we will have to put the best interests of people ahead of the multinationals and other vested interests.

What governments have done to date is initiate restructuring of a medical care system that masquerades as a health care system. Whether it is publicly funded, privately funded or a hybrid, the system is under siege. The changes are structural and are directed at controlling the cost of the system as opposed to initiating true health care reform. The individual, without recognizing it, is being forced to take personal responsibility for his or her own well-being.

In our current culture, responsibility for personal health has been abdicated to the professionals. For reform to take place, the individual must become the focal point of a "system of health." This means taking personal responsibility through everyday actions which will lead us to fundamental change and true reform.

Modern health care is focused on illness, disease and trauma. When something goes wrong, every attempt is made to fix it physically and usually at great cost. Only rarely are the psychological, emotional or spiritual aspects incorporated in the care-based system.

Unfortunately, major reformation is easier said than done because of the many and varied interests that make up the health care system. We, as a naive public and equally naive policymakers, tend to think the professionals that are in the system will somehow lead us to the enlightened territory that we covet. In my opinion, this is neither likely nor possible.

The reason I say this is because we are seeking a cultural shift. I believe this cultural shift can only come from outside the system. It begins with the policies that govern our educational and post-secondary institutions. It is these very institutions which perpetuate the illness and disease model around which Western medicine is built. It is impossible for a culture to change itself from within, which means that only an educated and enlightened public can force the needed reform that we seek.

The new continuum would be a "system of health" supported by education, alternative medicine and, finally, in time of crisis, the medical-care system.

To illustrate the need for change, and with all due respect, let me point out that doctors are considered experts in the fields of disability and nutrition. The irony is that they get virtually no training in disability of any kind and only minimal training in nutrition, which is usually the underlying cause of most illness and disease.

The Canadian Broadcasting Corporation (CBC) televised a feature titled "Teaching New Doctors Old Tricks" on its weekly program *The Nature of Things*, hosted by David Suzuki. The feature talked about the merits of allopathic and complementary medicine, their differences and benefits. A physiologist from the University of Toronto was interviewed and said, "Western medicine [allopathic] and surgery is only effective ten per cent of the time."

He went on to say that the other ninety per cent of the time it is really not very effective, particularly in treating chronic and degenerative conditions. The feature clearly demonstrated that in an emergency situation allopathic medicine, with its high technology and potent antibiotics, was the way to go. However, once an individual's condition has stabilized and he or she is on the mend, an array of complementary and alternative medical approaches are considerably more effective.

If this is true then it raises huge questions around the allocation of fiscal and human resources which taxpayers are concerned with more than politicians. Politicians become interested once the public tells them it is a priority.

World-famous author and lecturer Dr. Deepak Chopra, who has become known for his views on mind/body/soul medicine, has been quoted on several occasions as saying that he had once seen medicine as heroic. This was before he realized that all that he was doing was seeing patients one after another, and prescribing medication like a legalized drug pusher.

In his book *Return of the Rishi* he suggests that by purveying short-term cures but ignoring long-term prevention, the typical Western physician is fostering a diseased system and beyond that, a diseased world, with himself at its centre. The results of this diseased system can be similar to that of a spider entrapping a victim in its web.

In spite of the vast sums of money we are pouring into health care, we seem to be getting fewer results. We are losing the battle on many fronts, including such high-profile concerns as cancer and heart disease. This is at a time when our knowledge is at an all time high. This was eloquently explained as "The Health Paradox" in the book *Beyond Poverty and Affluence*, authored by Bob Goudzwaard and Harry de Lange.

Given the money we are spending and the knowledge we have, we could reasonably expect that our health should be improving rather than what is happening. If health care was a mutual fund portfolio we would have fired our investment managers long ago. In other words, our return on investment is extremely poor.

I have often asked myself the questions: Where, in the system, is the incentive to keep people healthy? Are the political risks and economic implications worth it? Are we as a society really serious about changing the system? I am hard pressed to come up with satisfactory answers. I am referring to our current system that we have inappropriately termed "health care." I can find all kinds of incentives to keep people ill or on the sick list, but I can't really find any incentives in the current system to keep people healthy beyond our own self initiative.

It seems to me that if there is an incentive it rests with the life insurance industry, workers' compensation boards, and in the US, possibly with Health Maintenance Organizations. However, the real reason they are interested is to control costs and maximize profits, not because they are really interested in keeping people healthy. In the case of the members of the insurance industry, their incentive doesn't present itself until they have sold a policy to you. The reason they were able to sell you the policy in the first place is because of the fear of an early death, a debilitating illness or injury, and not because there was an incentive to keep you healthy!

The financial rewards system for most doctors and other professionals in the social sciences often encourages dependency amongst those who are the recipients of service, and particularly the most vulnerable people in our society. Furthermore, we must reward people for promoting health and wellness, rather than what we are currently doing which is rewarding the promotion of illness and disease. Until we address the challenges in our current system head-on, we will always be subservient to the interests that have the power, money and control. The only real antidote is to take charge personally. This is where we have the power, if we only realize it.

I will add that, according to a senior official with the Centre For Disease Control in Atlanta, heart disease is estimated to be a $200 billion a year business (and growing) in the United States alone. In addition, in the last twenty years the American National Cancer Institute has spent $30 billion on cancer research. Even with this tremendous financial investment in these areas of health devastation we seem to be losing ground with our traditional approaches to research and its application. Could it be that our perverse system of financial compensation promotes illness rather than health?

To me the message is clear, and the message is, we must first take care of ourselves by taking care of our health. After that, the challenge is to change our systems and make them responsive to our collective needs so that they reflect a focus of wellness and well-being through a "system of health." This responsiveness must be reflected in our decisions and policies from cradle to grave. There are really no other options as we move forward in the fast-paced world in which we live. The alternatives are not very palatable, nor are they pleasant to contemplate, so let us begin by doing our part.

Most people fantasize about money and having lots of it, but if given a choice between being financially wealthy, or being mentally, emotionally and physically healthy, the choice for most of us is obvious. The former is not possible without the latter.

Ultimately, if we want people to take responsibility for their health, we must give them the tools. This means changing the culture and our whole approach to personal health. The next section begins by giving the individual permission to begin to affect change that starts with each and every one of us. In addition, it will give some practical information and tools that can make a difference on a daily basis.

Personal
Lessons
Learned

FACTORS AFFECTING OUR HEALTH

Virtually everything we do and everything around us can affect our health in some way. Basically, we can break it down to internal and external factors, combined with our related actions. The internal factors consist of the psychological, physical, emotional, mental and spiritual. All of these factors can be influenced and altered by our lifestyles, relationships and attitudes. The external factors can be anything from governmental policy to corporate actions, which have a whole range of factors in between. Today we are also dealing with the unknown effects of such influences as emissions from power lines and the long-term effects of chemical and antibiotic use, which all have the potential to negatively impact on our health. No doubt there are others, but these are the ones that come quickly to mind.

The obvious question is what can we control or affect? And if we can, how and what can we do as individuals? This is assuming, of course, that we want to influence our health and well-being.

Let us take a look at some of the lifestyle components that are somewhat obvious and often taken for granted or underrated in their importance to our daily health. They are addressed in no particular order of priority, but all are extremely relevant and work with a synergy that most people are not aware of. The harmony with which the human body works is truly amazing and is something to be supported by each one of us.

Most people seem to have a psychological block by thinking that there is a contradiction between having fun and leading a healthy lifestyle. It is possible to have it both ways and in the long run we should get more pleasure from the peace of mind that goes with it. This would go a long way to limiting the fact that so many major diseases are caused by poor lifestyle habits. Dr. Andrew Weil corroborated this perspective in his best-selling book *8 Weeks to Optimum Health.*

WHAT CAN WE CONTROL?

I believe we can significantly affect or even control, our hydration, breathing, diet, food intake, nutrition, exercise/activity, elimination of bodily waste/regularity, sleep and our belief systems. We are also responsible for what we give to others and society generally. Humour and fun in our lives are important, as is nourishing our emotional and spiritual needs.

If we take control of any or all of these areas we can have a significant effect on our personal health. Each area of our being is interdependent with another, and this is particularly relevant to our individual health. In order to affect change and ultimately take better control, we need to first become aware of what we can do and then make conscious changes.

When I decided to make conscious decisions about my health and lifestyle, that is when my life changed dramatically. I will attempt to share with you some of the things that made a difference in my life.

THE IMPORTANCE OF HYDRATION

"Oh, Dan can you see, that big green tree, where the water's running free, and waiting for you and me, cool clear water."
—From a song by The Sons of the Pioneers

When I first got polio I often didn't drink enough fluids, and particularly not enough water. The reason was because I was reliant on others to take me to the bathroom and it was a nuisance to continually need to ask for help. Often the help was not immediately available because there were more pressing needs that were being expressed by many of the other residents on the ward. This inconvenience often led to discomfort and the occasional bladder accident.

When I started dating I encountered many difficult and embarrassing situations because of my need to rely on others to take me to the bathroom. However, in reflecting on most of these situations I can say that the difficulties and embarrassment were self-induced. This self-induced difficulty was due to my reluctance to call on the willingness of others to help me with this basic bodily need which we all have.

Our entire world is fraught with contradiction and mine is, and was, no different. Like all young men, I secretly longed for certain members of the opposite sex to caress and fondle my most prized possession. And yet, when it came time to pee I would put myself through an inordinate amount of physical and emotional discomfort to avoid asking my date to help me in this uncomfortable moment of desired relief. I still don't know whether I was being considerate of my date, or being just plain stupid!

Since those early days of maturation I have collected enough pee stories to fill a book (another project on another day), some of them being very humourous. As an example, one evening I was asked out on a date by one of the women who worked on the polio ward where I lived. She was given two tickets to see Bobby Curtola at one of Edmonton's popular nightclubs and I was her date of choice for that evening. After imbibing and enjoying the performance, she helped me get into the van that was parked in the alley just behind the hotel where the show took place. The evening was still young, so it was too early to go home, but the problem was I had to pee. I eventually mustered up enough courage to ask my date to assist me in my moment of long awaited relief, after which she deposited the evidence on the ground under the rear of the van.

I was happy, but the best was yet to come. She tried to start the van without success and, being a damsel in distress with me in tow, there was a quick offer of assistance by a most unsuspecting gentleman. He approached our vehicle and offered his assistance by saying he couldn't help but notice our predicament. He went around the rear of the van and said, "I think I've found the problem." He continued by saying: "I think you have a leak," and before I could explain, he had stuck his finger in the evidence and quickly tasted it for substance before exclaiming; "It's not gas." I didn't have the heart to tell him the truth.

After all this, the vehicle started because it had only flooded, thus leaving us to enjoy the remainder of the evening; and all because I asked my date for her assistance.

The importance of drinking water became more apparent to me when some of my roommates began to experience problems with kidney stones. In those days the method of dealing with kidney stones was very uncomfortable and something that I wanted to avoid at virtually all cost. It was at this point that I stepped up my fluid intake and "be damned" with the resulting frequency! I think the increased consumption of water and juices was the beginning of major health changes for me, which didn't become apparent to me until much later in my life.

Once a person becomes aware of whatever it is that interests them, ensuing information presents itself. I remember reading a study in which the authors estimated that ninety per cent of all people walk around dehydrated simply because they don't drink enough water. They may drink large volumes of caffeinated beverages that often exacerbate the problems associated with dehydration, and in the process they fool themselves into thinking that they are actually drinking enough of the necessary fluids.

To further illustrate the point of the importance of hydration, I share a story that involved one of the top heart specialists at the University of Alberta Hospital. This occurred just a few short years after I ended my residency there. This physician was a long distance runner and was out training when he collapsed and died. The autopsy showed that he died of complications due to dehydration. This doctor was thirty-nine years old.

I cannot overstate the importance of drinking adequate amounts of water. A good rule of thumb to remember is that a person should consume half of their body weight in ounces. For example, if a person weighs 160 pounds he or she should consume approximately eighty ounces (ten eight-ounce glasses) of water daily. This will ensure a beneficial effect on all bodily functions. If at all possible, we should drink filtered water in order to remove unwanted substances. The advantage of filtering the water before ingesting it means that our body doesn't have to eliminate the unwanted substances such as chlorine, or any other accumulated foreign chemicals. Besides, most of us will notice an improvement in taste, in addition to knowing that we are doing something good for our bodies.

My wife Valerie can often measure her water intake simply by being cognizant of her level of energy because she finds it is often directly proportional to how much water she drinks. Most people need to cultivate a taste for water or remind themselves of the greater benefit of drinking more. Drinking larger quantities of water is something that we can do easily, while at the same time affecting our health in a meaningful way. It is also inexpensive, especially when we think of the alternative and the subsequent deterioration of our overall well-being which could result if dehydration persists.

In his book titled *Your Body's Many Cries for Water–You are not sick, You Are Thirsty!*, Dr. Fereydoon Batmanghelidj explains the body's thirst signals and the damage that occurs as a result of chronic dehydration. He states that "dry mouth" is the last outward sign of extreme dehydration. This is contrary to what most of us think.

Seventy-five per cent of our body is made up of water and eighty-five per cent of brain tissue is also water. When we consume water the brain is the first to be satisfied and the other organs are apportioned according to the amount of water that we drink. Dr. Batmanghelidj claims that the greatest health discovery of all times is that water is a natural medication for a variety of health conditions. He says, "Don't treat thirst with medications."

This is an excellent book (published by Global Health Solutions Inc., located in Falls Church, Virginia) and is a must-read for everyone, as water is what all of us are primarily made of, even if the nursery rhyme says sugar and spice!

BREATHING

Nobody needs to be told how important breathing is to our everyday existence, but most of us don't know or realize that it is the key to the completion of many important physical and psychological tasks. For example, weight-lifters find that proper breathing techniques make it possible to increase their ability to lift more weights. It is a key component of yoga as well as the martial arts. The intensity and tempo of our breaths can regulate our anxieties, relieving stress and providing significant health benefits.

Breathing is normally such a natural part of our being; however, it is something that I do with considerable difficulty when compared to the average person. I share the following story which took place at the fortieth birthday party of a good friend of mine. It involved a little boy named Scott who was four years old at the time. He was sitting about ten feet from me.

It must be remembered that I present a curious sight to some people and, in particular, children. This is due to both my wheelchair and obvious physical abnormalities. The great thing about children is that they aren't afraid to ask questions, nor beat around the bush when doing so. Scott was no exception.

The conversation went something like this:

"What happened to you?"

"Do you mean why am I in a wheelchair?" I inquired.

"Yes, why are you in a wheelchair?"

I explained that when I was nine years old I got polio, and that polio left me paralyzed, and now the wheelchair acts as my legs. I also asked him if he remembered getting vaccinations when he was younger, which he did. He kept looking at me and I knew he was going to ask another question.

"Why do you do this?" he asked, mimicking my gasps for air.

I should explain that when I breathe my jaw moves up and down. I responded to his question by explaining that when I was paralyzed my breathing muscles were also paralyzed, which meant that I couldn't breathe normally, in the way that he does. He seemed to accept my response. I then further explained that the method of breathing that I deployed was called "frog breathing."

He continued to study me and I knew that he was not finished asking questions.

"Are you a frog?"

My wife, who was within earshot, was heard to mutter under her breath, "No, he's just a horny old toad!"

For those of you who may be interested, the correct technical terminology is glossopharyngeal breathing, because it uses the muscles of the glossa (the tongue), and the pharynx (the throat). The term frog breathing is a slang term and is used because it involves a frog-like throat action. Frog breathing is a godsend for me, because without it I would need to use the respirator twenty-four hours a day. This skill which I have been able to master has been every bit as liberating for me as has been my wheelchair. Unfortunately, the skill of glossopharyngeal breathing is mainly used by people who have had polio, even though it has a much broader application.

I use frog breathing extensively to inflate my lungs, which does a couple of things for my health. It helps me cough and assists in minimizing congestion. Also, deep breathing acts like a vacuum cleaner in our bodies. In the process, it allows our lymphatic system to operate more efficiently.

I recommend that each of us do deep breathing exercises several times a day, which will virtually guarantee improved cardiovascular benefits. The increased oxygen intake alone will result in increased energy. The benefits will be multiplied if we combine deep breathing with other controllable health practices.

Even though breathing is part of our every move, it seems that we need to consciously deep-breathe on a regular basis in order to collect the resulting benefits. If you are experiencing lethargy or feeling tired on a regular basis, you may find breathing to be one of the keys to changing this negative factor in your life.

DIETARY HABITS

If you are like me, your eating habits were formed at a very young age. My mother was from London, England and came to Canada as a war bride. She brought with her the cultured tastes for roast beef, Yorkshire pudding, mashed potatoes and gravy and another old English favourite, fish and chips.

My father's family had as part of their staple diet such foodstuffs as eggs, cheese, butter and milk. It is entirely possible that this type of diet led to the premature deaths from heart disease of my birth father and two of his brothers.

Needless to say, I was like most children and didn't particularly like vegetables, especially when I learned that they were good for me! All of these were factors for me in my development, which became further complicated after I got polio.

After my birth father died my mother remarried, resulting in additional changes to the family diet based on individual preferences.

My parents were not very well off financially, which often meant making the most of whatever food and leftovers were available. This was a real challenge for mom and it tested her cooking creativity and skills in stretching the financial resources. Inherent in her creativity was the ability to daily provide the four food groups that were part of the Canada Food Guide at that time.

Two things I remember were that we always had two meatless days a week and we seldom drank pop. Both of these were factors in being able to stretch the family finances. The meatless days were influences my mother had gained during the war with one of the days being Friday, which was normally fish day (this must have been the Catholic influence even though we weren't Catholic). My mother was a great cook and she made even the most questionable meals tasty. Of course this sometimes meant using techniques which today are deemed less than desirable, because it often unknowingly involved an unhealthy fat content, but it sure tasted good.

It is against this backdrop that I entered hospital and I must admit, at best, the food in the University Hospital was less than tolerable for me. It always amazed me that people could actually get well in hospital in spite of the food!

My favourites were fried chicken drumsticks, deep fried fish, French fries, hot dogs, baloney sandwiches, mustard sandwiches and some desserts. Somehow, the cooks and the equipment they had to work with managed to dampen my interest in such previous favourites as hamburgers, roast beef and mashed potatoes. I think what ruined the taste of these delights was simply the poor quality of product compared to what I was used to, and not the capability of those who cooked the food.

The mashed potatoes were usually instant potatoes and one day I vividly recall biting into a big mouthful of potatoes and getting either what seemed to be toilet paper or the side of the instant potato box. This destroyed my interest in institutional mashed potatoes!

As I mentioned previously, my interest in vegetables was limited, and the exposure to the overcooked canned or frozen institutional vegetables did nothing to change my opinion. The only vegetable that I remember enjoying was corn. You can see that I was primarily a meat eater and for the most part my formative years involved poor nutrition which no doubt complicated my life, and particularly, my ability to eliminate properly.

That was then. Today is now, which finds me with dietary habits that are 180 degrees removed, when compared to yesteryear. My reasons for changing my dietary habits are due strictly to what makes me feel better and has little to do with religious or cultural beliefs.

The options available to us regarding diet are many and varied. What is optimal for one person is not necessarily appropriate for the next individual. This is something all of us would do well to remember, as most of us, at one time or another, have a tendency to think ours is either the best way or the only way. It has been said that no one is more critical of smoking or sensitive to smoke than reformed smokers. Maybe the analogy applies here!

All we can do is share our experiences and encourage each other to learn from them, leaving the individual to apply the information and lessons learned to his or her life. Because I have made such dramatic changes in my overall lifestyle, this is something I often need to remind myself of.

My big changes in dietary habits began when my brother Rody gave me the book titled *Fit For Life* by Marilyn and Harvey Diamond. The information in that book was the beginning of a magnificent journey for improved health. The principles of food combining made so much sense to me because I could recall times when my breathing was noticeably impaired, dependent upon when and what I ate. This may not be as important for others, but for me it was a very important revelation. My breathing was definitely affected by certain food combinations, which I was unaware of until I read this book.

I immediately put into practice the food combining principles regarding proteins and carbohydrates. I also started eating only fruit for breakfast, which improved my elimination efficiency. At this point I was still very much a meat eater, although I did such things as remove the skin from chicken (except for hot spicy chicken wings, my favourite!), and trimmed the excess fat from the rest.

By this time, my interest in fresh vegetables and salads had improved considerably. It was in my forty-ninth year that I became a vegetarian and, for the most part, also excluded milk and cheese. You might ask why I would do this, especially considering that I liked meat, cheese and milk. The reason was a simple one in that I felt much better and my system responded accordingly.

I remember thinking, how could anybody be vegetarian? Especially when vegetables tasted so awful. I guess the University Hospital experience was not a fair way to judge a lifestyle that involved vegetarianism! I also resented all the nurses acting as my mother, using such expressions as "Eat your vegetables; they are good for you." Another saying I remember is "Think of all the starving children in China and India." Neither one of them had any motivating effect on me; in fact it was probably the opposite. Thinking back, I was quite a contrary individual.

Little did I know that what I earlier despised would become a way of life for me and, eventually, hold a key to my energy and ability to provide for my family. I am thankful to the many teachers I have had along the way. I am also pleased that I was openminded enough to try new approaches, otherwise I may have missed out on significant benefits. Today I find myself healthier than I have ever been in my life and, for me, diet is one of the keys.

I continued to read everything that came my way regarding diet and the specifics that made for a healthy lifestyle. It was during this continued investigation that I discovered some aspects of eating meat that gave me a different perspective on what I was actually putting into my body.

It never really occurred to me that what we fed animals in the form of feed could affect our health. Besides the type of feed that farmers use, there is widespread use of antibiotics and chemicals, which also can affect our personal health. This does not even allow for the emotional strain that animals are put through in the whole process.

At first I didn't take this newfound information too seriously, probably because I was in denial due to the fact that I enjoyed eating meat. I then read that certain cultures will not eat food if the cook was stressed when preparing the meal. Also, the environment and climate that the animal was raised in prior to slaughter was often a major consideration.

It is widely accepted today that when we are stressed we shouldn't eat because our bodies are not in the proper state to accept the food. This means that it cannot utilize the nourishment as effectively or efficiently. Our North American lifestyle certainly is in conflict with this dietary principle. It must be remembered that we can always learn from others, and just maybe, stress, whether it is in our bodies or in that which we eat, can affect our health during food consumption.

There is no question in my mind that the mass production of foodstuffs, and the need to quench our economic thirst, has changed the quality of food and particularly meat. These changes are not always in our best health interests, even though they may be economically advantageous.

Life is often about making trade-offs and compromises. When it comes to food of any kind, we need to have a better awareness and understanding regarding where we draw the line. It applies to more than just environmental concerns, which usually get our attention when it comes to economic trade-offs.

For example, several articles have been written detailing the growing public concern about the use of chemicals and antibiotics in the agricultural sector and their negative effect on humans.

Health Canada has been routinely accused of approving drugs for agricultural use without asking questions, or even ignoring the possible long-term effects. This has forced the Federal Government's Auditor General's Department to examine Health Canada's drug approval process.

The super resistant strains of bacteria that are now presenting themselves could have undesirable effects that we can't even begin to contemplate. For a person like myself with respiratory requirements, or a person with other health considerations, this can be frightening or even devastating. Ultimately, it will affect each and every one of us in some way during our lifetime.

Regardless of beliefs around the consumption of meat, whether they be religious, cultural or personal, there is a worsening problem around the growing, preparation and handling of what is a mainstay of most North Americans' diets. The most obvious action that we can personally take is to look for a clean source of meat, or not eat what we are being force-fed, so to speak. The only way that policies and approaches will change is if we get the attention of the decision-makers. These choices may seem to be extreme, but what are our alternatives?

It really comes down to health and where it fits in terms of our personal priorities. We can no longer look only to the authorities to make our decisions for us, because the information is voluminous and changes regularly. We as individuals need to become more aware and knowledgeable in order to influence our health.

DAIRY PRODUCTS

The subject of dairy products can be a very sensitive one because it has the tendency to raise the ire of the dairy industry. To give you an idea of just how sensitive this subject can be; the late Dr. Charles Attwood was speaking in Saskatoon, Saskatchewan while promoting his book *Dr. Attwood's Low-Fat Prescription For Kids*. Following his speech, Dr. Attwood was accosted by an irate dairy farmer who accused Dr. Attwood of trying to put farmers like him out of business. Dr. Attwood told the farmer that this was not his intent, but he would be negligent if he didn't share his knowledge and the research that he had done with the public so that others could make an informed decision.

The information that is now available from notable medical and scientific authorities has challenged assumptions that we had long taken for granted. As we learn more we will need to make individual and societal choices based on, either, economics and politics, or based on what is best for people and their collective health. These are difficult choices and will be part of the new paradigm of health, or "system of health" that I spoke about earlier.

Without meaning to pass judgment, I have made changes in my consumption of dairy products. These changes have significantly contributed to my improved health, especially with regard to respiratory tract infections. Many health practitioners now believe that a significant portion of the population just cannot handle or properly digest milk products. In contrast, some Ayurveda medical practitioners say that it is the way that people drink milk which creates the problems, and not the milk itself. Ayurveda recommends that people first boil milk before drinking it in order to get the best results. Alternatively, we should drink it warm or at room temperature. They also suggest that milk be ingested on its own (or with something sweet) rather than with other foods.

At this point I wish to share some information I gleaned from a newsletter titled *New Century Nutrition* (Volume 2, No. 5 May 1996) which is published in Ithaca, New York. The contributors to this newsletter are respected worldwide for their contribution to the fields of medicine, health and nutrition.

In responding to a question about osteoporosis, the late Dr. Benjamin Spock essentially said that if an individual consumes excessive animal protein it will add to calcium loss, even if the source of the protein is dairy products. This occurs through the process of acidification of the blood by protein, which in turn causes the kidneys to excrete calcium.

Dr. Spock said that he had become convinced that meat and dairy products could be greatly reduced or even eliminated, as long as a person was eating lots of vegetables, fruits, whole grains and legumes. Dr. Spock practised pediatrics and wrote eleven books. Dr. Spock's *Baby and Child Care* has been translated into thirty-nine languages since the time of its publication fifty years ago.

In the same issue, in an article entitled "The Great American Milk Myth," Dr. Charles Attwood corroborates Dr. Spock's perspective, pointing out that it is calcium balance that is important. Calcium balance is the relationship between the intake and loss of this important mineral and calcium is what determines bone density.

According to Dr. Attwood, the true connection between milk, strong bones and good teeth, isn't exactly what the dairy industry has been telling us all these years. This is because it has more to do with calcium balance than the amount of calcium that an individual consumes. Dr. Spock and Dr. Attwood both make the point that the problem with milk and other dairy products is that they are not only rich in calcium, but protein which has been shown to create calcium loss through the urinary tract.

Dr. Attwood's research reveals that, generally speaking, if you eat a plant-based diet you'll get as many total calories as if you ate meat and dairy products. In other words, calorie for calorie, vegetables are better sources of calcium than milk and cheese. It's the whole meal that counts.

An area of diet and nutrition that has always been confusing for me is the issue of fats. Descriptive labels such as "unsaturated," "saturated," "mono-unsaturated" and "poly-unsaturated" have all been very confusing to me at one time or another. To clarify, fatty acids are the individual components of oils in the same way that amino acids are the building blocks of proteins. The two classes of fatty acids are saturated and unsaturated.

Essential oils are to plants what blood is to the human body and are rich in both oxygen and nutrients. Essential oils distribute oxygen and nutrients throughout the plant in the same way that blood carries oxygen and nutrients to the various organs and cells in the human body.

In one of his health seminars, Dr. Humbart (Smokey) Santillo (the creator of Juice Plus+) covered the subject of fats. He separated fats into those which are "good" and those which are "bad." He basically challenged and labelled as misinformation most of what we have been led to believe about fats and calories in our daily diet. He helped clear up some of the confusion for me in this highly controversial area of dietary and health information.

Essentially, he says that we need a proper balance of good fats to remain healthy and to have a strong immune system. He also talked about studies such as the well-known Framingham Heart Study (a renowned twenty-year project involving one thousand men between the ages of forty-five and sixty-five), and how those researchers have proven that high cholesterol levels are not necessarily caused by high fat intake. Apparently, it has more to do with how the body can or can't use these fats once they are ingested.

Further analysis of data from this same study by a research team from Harvard Medical School found that a three per cent rise in total fat consumption reduced the risk of a stroke by fifteen per cent. However, it is still widely believed by most doctors and researchers that saturated fat is the least healthy type of fat to eat because of a perceived link with heart disease.

Of course the effects of fats ingested into our body will be influenced by the combinations and amounts of carbohydrates, sugars, absorbable calcium, proteins and other such elements that we ingest. The results we get in the form of weight gain or weight loss, will also be affected by the amount of fats, carbohydrates and sugars that our body burns due to physical exertion.

It has been helpful for me to know that unsaturated fats (so-called good fats) are liquid at room temperature and are cold-pressed oils such as canola, olive, sesame, flax and fish oils. Other types of good fats are avocado, butter, nuts and seeds. The essential omega-3 and omega-6 fatty acids are grouped into this category. These are good fats because they are metabolized into anti-inflammatory substances. It is important to understand that these are essential oils. Our body must have essential oils to remain healthy and to avoid diseases such as cardiovascular disease.

Saturated fats (so-called bad fats) are usually unsaturated fats that have been nutritionally damaged. This includes hydrogenated fats, hydrogenated oils and other such products that have been homogenized or undergone damage through the cooking and preparation process. Examples would include margarine, lard, shortening and most vegetable oils. These are the harmful fats that are metabolized into inflammatory substances. It is important to read labels and for us to understand that the terms hydrogenated and homogenized are, for the most part, indicative of unhealthy processes.

I encourage you to study this issue of fats more closely.

NATURE'S ENERGY

Fruits

Fruit is a food that virtually everybody likes unless they have developed an allergy of some sort. It is also the only food that gives you energy almost immediately. It takes little effort on the part of the body's digestive system so, consequently, fruit is readily available to the body as an energy source. All other foods take considerably longer to digest and, as a result, take energy away from the body in the short term. I was amazed to learn that digestion was the number two energy drain on the body. For those who are interested, sex is number one. Depending on an individual's sex life, digestion may be the number one energy drain!

Fruits are the cleansers of the body and play a very important role in assisting our elimination system. In order for fruit to work its cleansing magic in an optimal way, it should be eaten on its own twenty to thirty minutes before eating a more substantial meal. If fruit is eaten following a regular meal, or as a snack, it is best to eat it approximately three hours following a meal.

I wasn't sure about this principle but, as part of my personal philosophy, I believed the best way to learn was to try it. I found it works for me and you may want to consider incorporating it into your daily routine. It takes little effort and may be effective for you, so why not try it?

Eating a variety of fruits and vegetables is very important because the properties in them work together in a complementary manner. For example, the vitamin C of an orange is different from the vitamin C of a kiwi fruit once it is ingested into the body. The reason is that there are complementary properties in each of the different fruits that work in synergy allowing the vitamin C, or other vitamins, to work their magic in an effective and efficient manner once they enter the human body. This is the main reason that man will never be able to duplicate nature when it comes to the magic of fruits and vegetables.

There are so many nutrients and enzymes that it is unlikely that we will discover all of them in your lifetime or mine, or exactly how they work together. We are just now beginning to have an understanding of their role in preventing and healing illness and disease. All fruits are different, even though they may contain some of the same nutrients. When we eat them we don't know the exact nature of what we are eating, we just know that they are good for us.

The different coloured fruits present a way of knowing that we are getting different nutrients and promise to keep scientists busy for a long time as they try to figure out their application for humankind. Also, the different colours suggest to us that we need a variety of different fruits in order to benefit in the way nature intended. It is not possible today to pick up a newspaper or magazine without seeing information telling us to eat up to five servings of different fresh fruits daily.

Before leaving the subject of fruit, my reading has led me to believe that the mega-doses of certain vitamins such as vitamin C may have some beneficial effect on our bodies, but they are not nearly as effective as the real thing. The reason is that sixty mg of vitamin C from fresh fruit, in all likelihood, is much more effective when ingested into our body than taking 500 mg of a vitamin C supplement tablet. It is the synergistic properties in the fresh fruit that makes the sixty mg more effective. You can put gas in the car but it won't run without oil, which is a comparative analogy to what happens with fruit and, for that matter, vegetables.

Vegetables

If fruits are the cleansers of the body, then vegetables are the builders. Vegetables are similar to fruits in that they come in a variety of shapes, sizes and colours (sounds like people, doesn't it?).

Science is just now discovering that vegetables and their contained properties in the form of vitamins, minerals, enzymes, phytochemicals, soluble and insoluble fibre, antioxidants and anything else they have yet to discover, in all likelihood, hold the key to our health. There is a great deal of research that is beginning to yield supportive evidence for this statement.

The interest that the power of fruits and vegetables are catalyzing is about to emerge into something that could parallel the pharmaceutical industry. From a business perspective, the interest in nutriceuticals and foodaceuticals has taken off. There is a race to see who can get to the financial finish line first, or at least, be part of the pack that gets there.

FOOD AND SCIENCE

This interest in fruits and vegetables is good news for consumers and people who are interested in taking responsibility for and control of their health. The biggest problem that I see with this industry, is that man, led by scientists and researchers, is always trying to duplicate or mimic nature.

The factors of which I speak are that man, in all probability, will never be able to duplicate nature when it comes to understanding what properties fruits and vegetables contain, how these properties work in synergy, or in what proportion or quantities nature provides. It is similar to any recipe: once you change one ingredient or its quantity, the taste and effect changes. The thing with fruits and vegetables is that nature's recipe and ingredients are put together with a complexity and synergy that only the powers of the universe can begin to comprehend.

The business of combining science and food has exploded into a multi-billion-dollar bonanza for large businesses and national economies. Through the process of genetic engineering, many crops are being altered to withstand their natural enemies. This is resulting in many changes in the agricultural and food industries. Also, it is raising some poignant questions regarding efficacy and safety with regard to consumption.

It is becoming almost impossible to determine whether we are eating genetically altered food or food that was grown under normal farming practices. Most labels do not declare that food has been genetically altered or that it may be a combination of one or more species of product. This whole area of science and food is beginning to create tensions internationally between European and North American interests. European interests are concerned with safety and health while North American interests seem to be more focused on profits and the effect on the economy.

The point is that you and I may not even know what we are eating, nor is it necessarily possible to find out. We are forced to rely on governments, industry and the scientific community to look after this important area that affects us on a daily basis. The best thing we can do is to become as informed as time and information permits.

Enzymes

There is a great deal of interest in what enzymes and phytochemicals can do for our health. Although we, as an enlightened public, don't necessarily need to know the details of how these natural properties work, it is definitely to our advantage to have some understanding of the importance of enzymes. At a minimum, we should know that they are prevalent in raw foods, particularly fruits and vegetables, and are vital to our well-being. Enzymes have been described as the essence of life itself and can be considered the workhorse of life. Briefly, enzymes are essential for every metabolic process that takes place within our body. This includes thinking and any other internal or external body activity that may take place, whether we are asleep or awake. Most importantly, enzymes are responsible for digesting the food that we eat. And, it is the quality of digestion that determines how efficiently we can convert food and its nutrients into useful fuel for the body. They also are important to the elimination of waste which is a natural by-product of digestion.

Research has been going on into the effects of enzymes since the 1930s and may be the most studied phenomenon in the human body. Even though this is the case, the results and their beneficial effects on our health have not been very widely discussed or publicized.

Research is continuing to discover new enzymes that play a variety of catalytic roles in our bodily functions. The digestive enzymes that are contained in raw fruits and vegetables allow us to digest food properly and to use the energy that is contained in these gifts of nature. A benefit to eating raw fruits and vegetables is that the digestive enzymes contained in them assist in preserving the natural store of enzymes in our bodies. The less raw fruits and vegetables we eat, the more we have to draw on the body's ability to generate and replace the required enzymes for digestion. In more recent days, I have been taking digestive enzymes in capsule form with my lunch and evening meal, and I have noticed the benefits. The benefits include less bloating and better elimination.

Dr. Edward Howell's studies show that the body has a genetically determined and finite enzyme potential which is gradually depleted throughout the aging process. His research also suggests that the rate of enzyme depletion in the body is a determining factor in longevity. Enzyme depleted foods rob the body of its enzyme potential and reduces life span. This means that the organs (such as the pancreas) that produce the needed digestive enzymes must work harder, therefore, leading to illness, disease and premature aging. Research is proving that it is possible to prevent illness and disease (such as heart and cancer) and even slow the aging process through dietary habits.

Phytochemicals

Phytochemicals have generated interest in that they are believed to hold a vital key to the prevention of illness and disease. These are natural occurring substances and science is beginning to understand how they may impact on a variety of illnesses and disease. What are phytochemicals? Phytochemicals are bio-active compounds that are found in certain plants. Research into phytochemicals and the beneficial effects of fruits and vegetables is ongoing. The result of a major cancer study that was recently released in the US was singing the praises of eating fruits and vegetables.

This information regarding fruits and vegetables shouldn't be a surprise. In 1994, Mindy Hermann, RD wrote an article in *McCalls* magazine, entitled, "The Healing Power of Fruits and Vegetables." In that article she talked about the beneficial properties of phytochemicals. She surmised that phytochemicals seemed to work their magic by interfering with the development of cancer at the cellular level.

The beneficial effects of phytochemicals are not limited to cancer. According to Dr. Roby Mitchell, MD, who publishes his own newsletter titled, *News for Your Health*, cancer isn't the only target of their nutritional weapons. He believes some types of phytochemicals may forestall diabetes and reduce the risk of heart disease, while others may block infectious diseases by boosting the immune system.

Scientists and researchers will be uncovering for some time to come the secrets of Nature's energy which is naturally contained in raw fruits and vegetables. Understanding this information is important. The use of this information by individuals, scientists, researchers and the medical profession is another story!

The message is clear—we must eat a variety of more raw fruits and vegetables in order to be healthy. Many medical authorities are now recommending that we need a minimum of five to ten servings daily. I ask you the reader, what do you think would happen to your health if you did this on a daily basis?

Cooking Fruits and Vegetables

Briefly, I want to explain that when we cook vegetables and process fruits, we can actually destroy or damage many of the valuable nutrients. The digestive enzymes contained in raw fruits and vegetables are destroyed and rendered useless when we cook them at a certain temperature (above 118° F). A most unfortunate characteristic of the foods we eat in our modern world is that the methods used in storing, preserving and preparing foods kill the enzymes that are naturally found in the food. Baking, boiling, stewing, frying, microwaving and irradiation (food radiation) all completely destroy the enzymes in food. The majority of our food intake is either cooked or processed. This means that the body must provide these enzymatic properties from its natural stores.

The human body and digestive system were not designed to consume cooked food. Enzymes occurring in raw food aid in digestion so that your body's enzymes do not have to do all the work of digestion. When you eat raw food, chewing releases the enzymes in the food to begin digestion. Then the food sits in your stomach for nearly an hour before your body's digestive enzymes are secreted. It is during this time that the food enzymes do their work in breaking down the complex food molecules of protein, carbohydrates, fats and fibre.

When enzymes are missing from your food, the full burden of digestion falls on your digestive system. Dr. Howell's research has proven that a diet of cooked foods causes rapid premature death in mice and that the speed of premature death is directly connected to the temperature at which the food is cooked.

Day to day living puts a tremendous demand on your body's supply of enzymes. Cooked and processed foods, caffeinated and alcoholic beverages, colds and fevers, pregnancy, stress, strenuous exercise and extreme weather conditions are just some of the things that use up your enzymes at a rapid rate.

The digestion of enzyme-deficient food is an extremely energy-consuming task. This is why we often feel tired after a big meal. Fatigue, constipation, gas, heartburn, headaches, bloating and colon problems are just a few of the many conditions that can be caused by poor digestion. Research tells us that the body's ability to produce enzymes decreases as we grow older and, at the same time, tissue break down and chronic health conditions increase.

The connection may be subtle, but nevertheless there is a connection to the strength of the immune system and the depleting reserves of the body. The way to strengthen and fortify our bodies and our health is to treat what we eat with respect and understanding. In order to do this, we all need to read and learn from nature and from each other.

When we cook our food, we should do so using the least destructive method. By way of example, two methods we can use are gently stir frying or lightly steaming our vegetables. The other thing we can remember, as a rule of thumb, is that the more preparation that goes into food before we eat it, the less nutritious it becomes. Cooking, pasteurization and processing basically renders enzymes ineffective due to damage and, therefore, they become inactive or, for all intents and purposes, dead. If we are aware of these factors we will be in a position to make healthier choices when it comes to cooking and eating food.

Fibre

The two types of fibre that we know of are soluble and insoluble. The insoluble fibre is known as the "scrubbers." These scrubbers cleanse our colon and are contained in a variety of foods, including fruits and vegetables. Thinking back, I hardly ever ate fibre until my mother started helping me with my bowel movements by making me some delicious bran muffins!

Soluble fibre is absorbed into the blood stream and plays an important role in cleaning our arteries and assisting in eliminating waste from our bodies. Soluble fibres are most prevalent in fruits and vegetables. This is one of the main reasons that fruits and vegetables are believed to be so effective in assisting with minimizing the risk of, or in healing, heart disease and cancer.

WEIGHT MANAGEMENT

When I was going through the acute phase of rehabilitation it required a lot of energy. I recognized early in my life that it was important to keep my weight down to a manageable level; in fact, at times I became almost obsessed with it. I was not unlike the teenage girl of today, always concerned about diets even when I didn't need to be. I eventually got over the obsession, but nonetheless realized that keeping my weight under control was absolutely essential in order for me to have the quality of life I wanted for myself. I believe that the issue of weight management combined with the importance of energy, are two of the most important and essential elements of health.

Fortunately for me, even though I learned about nutrition and a healthy lifestyle later in life, my weight was always manageable. This made it easy to go places, do things and have people who were willing to assist me. Over the years, I had several roommates who found themselves battling weight problems, which often denied them many opportunities for socialization and enjoyment.

The importance of weight management was magnified when I started dating and began to lead a so-called quasi-normal existence in relation to the opposite sex. I say quasi-normal because an institutional environment, such as the hospital I grew up in, was not conducive to, nor supportive of, intimate interaction. By having my weight under control, it allowed me to go places with the women in my life who were willing to assist me with my physical needs. This was necessary because of my dependency on others for several of my daily physical requirements.

Overeating

Something that is worth being aware of is that overeating is due to more than just putting too much food into our mouth at one sitting. It has a lot to do with our need to feel full or satisfied after eating. If we are eating a diet that is deficient in nutrients for our needs, we are going to feel hungry. The reason is, the body's sensory system dealing with food intake can only use the nutrients from the food that we put into our bodies and the rest it must eliminate. In reality, our body can only use a very small proportion of the food that we eat because most of what we ingest results in waste.

For example, it takes approximately one and a half pounds of raw carrots to make a six-ounce glass of fresh carrot juice. If you take this further, quoting the most notable authority on juicing, Jay Kordich (The Juice Man), "When we eat, our body only utilizes about twelve per cent of the nutritional value of a carrot and the rest is eliminated."

This means that in order to get the same benefit from eating raw carrots as we would from drinking a six-ounce glass of fresh carrot juice, we would have to eat about fifteen pounds of carrots!

This blew me away when I heard it, but it did drive home the point about what the body can actually use after ingesting food. Since then, I have taken an avid interest in juicing and its benefits. If juicing is something you are not currently doing, it would be well worth your while to investigate the potential benefits.

When eating foods that have been cooked, and depending on how long they have been cooked and at what temperature, even less of the nutrients are available to our body. When we combine this with the fact that we only use a small percentage of them after ingestion, it often leaves the body craving more. What we normally do to satisfy this craving is eat more food, but it has been proven that if we eat more nutritious meals we actually feel the need to eat less food, while at the same time getting more nutritional benefit.

Therefore, if we eat more food because we feel hungry after having a big meal, we should remember that we are not really hungry in the sense that we need more food, but we are hungry in the sense that we need more nutrition. Most North Americans, for a variety of reasons, don't eat properly. Is it any wonder that we are experiencing more heart disease and cancer than ever before, even though we as a society possess more knowledge than ever before?

One of the things that we can all do is to learn more about healthy eating. In doing so, we will be able to address the problems associated with overeating. These problems include obesity and its complications. The key is not the quantity of food that we eat but the quality. The quality is what affects the body's ability to use the nutrients, thus affecting whether we feel hungry or not.

Chewing

It seems almost hypocritical of me to be suggesting to you that you should consider chewing your food better and longer for maximum benefit. Admittedly, I have the same problem as you in that we both live in a fast-paced existence which results in swallowing before chewing properly. However, unlike you, I have an additional problem in that the longer I chew the more difficult it becomes for me to breathe, due to my respiratory difficulties.

The moment we put food into our mouths is the moment that the digestive process begins. The more we chew our food before swallowing, the less wear and tear on the body's organs that are involved in further digestion. It also means that the longer we chew the slower we will eat. The slower we eat, the more time the body will have to utilize the nutritional components that have been broken down through better chewing. In other words we will get more mileage per bite (mpb). Maybe these words from Mahatma Ghandi sum it up: "We must chew our drink and drink our food."

This further means that because our digestive system is operating more optimally, our cravings for more food will decrease, and therefore, as a natural consequence we will feel less of a need to satisfy hunger through increased food intake. Also, it takes a few minutes for the message of being satisfied to get to the hunger control centre in our bodies from our stomachs. By chewing our food longer our systems can benefit.

The domino effect of not chewing our food properly, eating too fast and improper digestion leads to eating larger quantities. For many people, this will result in being overweight and having less energy, thus impacting their activity levels and ultimately their health. Chewing is not normally thought of as being a big factor in weight control and health, but it is. The great thing about realizing this is that we can do something immediately by chewing our food properly. For most of us, this will result in better absorption of nutrients, less food intake, better health, and not only that, it will save us money.

Malnutrition

Malnutrition is a condition that we normally associate with third world countries but it is more prevalent in North America than we think. The reason is that as a populace we are eating food that is less than nutritious because of our hectic, stress-filled lives, and our love affair with fast food.

We also think of malnutrition when we think of not getting enough to eat, which is why we consider it a third world problem. This is true, but it is possible to take in what might appear to be adequate quantities of food and still be malnourished. This is what is happening in our North American society. This is due to the poor quality of food that a large number of us are eating on a regular basis.

Because I was a big hamburger lover, I know I had to make a conscious effort to eat less at fast food restaurants. Even now it is a big temptation to take our children to them because of the heavy advertising, peer influence and the convenience. I must admit that sometimes we give in to these pressures, even though we know better.

If you are a parent or grandparent, you would probably find Dr. Charles Attwood's book interesting and informative reading. It contains information that we all should be aware of if we are serious about positively impacting our societal health.

In his book, *Low-Fat Prescription for Kids*, he talks about our future, namely children, and what we are doing to them without realizing it. He speaks in a direct, forthright and provocative manner, including how our eating habits are for the most part ingrained in us by the time we are eight years old.

IMPORTANT FUNCTIONS

Exercise and Activity

Until my wheel-a-thon experience that I described earlier, exercise was something that I thought was for other people. After this experience it became a part of my regular routine. I attempted to incorporate either wheeling on the indoor or outdoor track at the University of Alberta, or riding the stationary exercise bike we have at home. I continue to do this three or four times a week to maintain my level of fitness. I believe that this physical activity has helped me with my stamina, breathing and mental focus. All three of these elements are important in my life.

Sport has always been a big part of my life. Before getting polio I loved competing in track and always looked forward to the track and field days we used to have at our school in the Yukon. I think winning the ribbons for first, second or third place was probably very important for me because I loved to compete.

After getting polio my attention shifted from one of competing to one of being an interested spectator in many sports. My favourites were football and hockey, the latter because I was fortunate as a youngster to visit the dressing room of the pro hockey team that was in Edmonton in the mid 1950s. This was a big thrill for me and probably was an influence in solidifying my interest in team sports. The football influence came from my roommates, who knew more about the game than I did at the time, but I learned and later became an expert in my own mind!

As I grew to adulthood I was looking for ways to become more involved in community activities. Sport administration seemed like a natural way to do it, based on the experience I had gained in my life to that point.

After leaving Jaycees I became involved in the wheelchair sport movement in a big way. I started as the president of the local Paralympic Sports Association and remained in that position for two and a half years before joining the Canadian Wheelchair Sports Association as its executive director in 1974. I remained involved with CWSA for the better part of the next twenty years in a variety of roles, including four two-year terms as president.

Between 1978 and 1987, I was also extensively involved in managing and developing the Alberta Northern Lights Wheelchair Basketball Society in Edmonton. During my stints with these various organizations, combined with my voluntary experiences with the 1978 Commonwealth Games and the 1983 World University Games, I learned a great deal about competition, exercise and physical activity in general.

I also coached and managed a mixed slo-pitch team for eighteen years and we won our share of tournaments. In addition, I managed the Canadian Men's Wheelchair Basketball Team to the 1979 and 1983 World Championships. These were excellent learning opportunities for me.

I learned that to be active was very important and that physical activity was a key component of a healthy lifestyle. Looking back at what I remember is interesting, not in the nostalgic sense but for what it reveals by way of reflection.

Athletes train hard, make significant personal sacrifices and do all kinds of other things to improve their personal athletic performance, including bending the rules. However, the majority of high performance athletes do not pay enough attention to their dietary and fluid intake. There is no question in my mind that the performances of many athletes could be improved significantly, just by incorporating some of the suggestions contained in this book into their daily dietary regimen. That is to say nothing of what they could accomplish with additional nutritional counselling that is specific to their athletic activity.

For us, as the average Joe, it is important to maintain a certain level of physical activity, if possible, in order to help our body systems to operate effectively and with efficiency. Most of us approach physical activity without a plan, or even a goal, but rather with the intention that we are going to do something healthy for ourselves. This is noble, but can be problematic for people who don't know what they are doing to themselves.

In a guest column titled, "No Body's Perfect," in the newsletter *New Century Nutrition*, Amy Lanou, PhD asked the question: What is the American stereotypical ideal body for men and women? She surmised that for most Americans, being thin, fit and beautiful is synonymous with love, success and power. If her analysis is correct, it means we North Americans believe physical beauty holds the promise of eternal happiness. This includes many people believing that the rest of their lives would automatically fall into place if they could reach a certain weight or have their nose modified. In the article, Dr. Lanou referenced a recent national survey that found more women feared becoming fat than feared dying.

This perspective is further amplified through the results of recent research that was done in both England and Canada. The study revealed that teenage girls are more likely to take up smoking believing that it will help them lose weight or stay thin. They know that smoking is not good for their health, but they are more concerned about being overweight, becoming fat or damaging their figure.

Why is this? How is the ideal body image shaped? The answer of course is through the media and by advertisers. The slick images that are presented to us help to perpetuate, shape and reinforce an image that bears little resemblance to the reality of our daily lives. Why are we taken in by these smooth promotions? The reason is simple, because beauty sells, and we buy.

Is it necessary to meet this ideal to be healthy? The answer is clearly "No." People of many sizes, shapes, weights and facial features are very healthy and fit. The reason is because health is connected to lifestyle factors and not to appearance.

If possible, it is wise to get some advice from people who understand physical activity and exercise. The reason we should seek advice is because each one of us is different in stature and in nature. Also, we often have different reasons for what we are doing; we may need a specific program tailored to our wants and needs.

Even though individuals may have pre-existing conditions, this does not necessarily preclude them from taking part in a regular physical activity program. It does mean that it is important to get good advice and direction. My motto is "moderation is the key," and be consistent in the process.

I have taken the time to observe and study a number of people who I think are models when it comes to preserving their health and vitality. Some of those people are not physically able to do physical exercise in the same way others are. However, there is a myriad of programs that are available to virtually everyone who has any physical capability. An example of such programs exists at the University of Alberta Faculty of Physical Education and Sport Studies. The facility, founded and directed by my friend Dr. R. D. (Bob) Steadward, caters to people with various physical disabilities, and offers excellent programs that are designed specifically for the individual participant's needs.

If physical exercise is not an option for some people, activity is an option for everybody. I believe that it is as important, if not more important, to exercise your brain through a variety of activities and interests, as it is to exercise your physical body. I know people who have maintained a healthy existence in spite of being totally dependent on others for most of their physical needs. They have accomplished this level of health through maintaining an active interest in not only their own lives, but by taking an interest in other people. It suggests to me that we human beings are meant to be active.

The Elimination of Bodily Waste
"The Greeks idealized the human body; we treat it as little better than an animated garbage can."

—Dr. Robert Jackson,
The Fattening Regime: A Manual for the Too-Thin (1928)

Every function that our body carries out is vital and interdependent. There is no function that is more important than the elimination of waste from our bodies. I cannot overstate this point.

Elimination is referred to in many different terms, some of which are crude and not very respectful of this important bodily process. No matter how we refer to this natural occurrence, it plays a significant role in our overall health. This is something few of us ever think about. I suggest that if we paid more attention to our elimination system, we would experience many positive health benefits.

I speak from firsthand experience. I took laxatives and used manual assistance to eliminate for the first sixteen years that I lived in the hospital. This was an extremely uncomfortable period in my life. Needless to say, enemas and the manual removal of stool from my bowel were extremely uncomfortable. These experiences contain many unpleasant memories for me. First of all, I was very young and my orifice was not used to this supposedly necessary abuse!

Because of my inability to eliminate properly, I experienced a great deal of gas and often needed a rectal tube to give me some relief. I remember my first Halloween in hospital like it was yesterday, because it was both a pleasant and unpleasant experience at the same time. At this stage in my rehabilitation I was unable to sit up for any length of time, and at any rate I didn't as yet have my own wheelchair. I was unable to breathe on my own for more than a couple of minutes at a time, so I needed to be ventilated with a hand-held device, while at the same time being pushed around the hospital on a stretcher.

I don't remember who helped me. However, I do know whoever it was worked extremely hard and that they must have been multi-talented. I do remember that individual brought a lot of joy to a young boy who was experiencing a great deal of discomfort due to extreme gas and bloating. For some reason, I remember getting some relief from having a five-pound sandbag placed across my abdomen. The great news about that evening was that we made a big haul in the form of junk food! Hey, it tasted better than hospital food. When I first started taking laxatives they were quite strong in dosage. Gradually, over the years, I was able to decrease the dosage and also the type of laxative that I needed to take. When I was taking the stronger type of laxative it sometimes resulted in the opposite of constipation and I would need to frequent the bathroom. Sometimes I didn't get there on time, which presented a whole set of embarrassing and unwanted circumstances. I was extremely pleased to eventually regain control of my bowel movements, which no doubt was another big change point in my life.

Being able to reduce and eventually eliminate the use of laxatives from my nightly routine, correlated directly with my improved dietary habits and the drinking of more water. Initially, I must admit that my improved eating habits were more by accident than design. Looking back, I see where the changes in my eating habits and lifestyle in general were incremental, and these changes gradually resulted in health benefits for me. Someone was looking over me, because these positive changes that were occurring seemed to be a result of good fortune more than good planning.

When my roommates and I moved to the Aberhart Centre from the University Hospital it proved to be a very positive move for all of us, in many different ways. One of the more significant benefits was better food and more choices. I think the main reason for this was that the Aberhart was a facility that was built to house and look after people with tuberculosis. Diet and quality food were part of the treatment for this population. The fact that the facility was smaller and more responsive to the needs of its residents also helped.

The food was not only better but the entire atmosphere was more amenable to enjoying meals, because there were fewer rules and less pressure to adhere to fixed schedules. By the time we moved to the Aberhart I was eating out quite often. This was because I had become more active in the community outside the Aberhart and I happened to be away at meal times more often than not. As a result, I probably wound up eating healthier and more varied food.

The other factor was that I had discovered women, and some of them even responded to me in an encouraging fashion. This interaction with the opposite sex resulted in several choices that wound up impacting my health, both physically and emotionally!

The whole point of this section is to impress upon you that healthy eating by way of nutritious meals and drinking lots of water will dictate the results you get with the elimination of waste from your body. What is the big deal about elimination anyway? Why is it so important to our health?

Earlier on I mentioned that our body uses a very small percentage of the food and its nutrients. That means that our body needs to eliminate the rest through our elimination system. Specifically, through the skin, the lungs, the urinary tract or the bowel.

Most of the waste should be taken care of through the urinary tract and the bowel. This is the case when we eat good food and when we digest our food properly. The digestive system alone is a phenomenal work of art with its ability to extract nutrients and energy efficiently from the food we eat. However, once we've swallowed our food, we often ignore the rest of the process. If we don't digest our food properly and use it as fuel for our needs, it will be turned into toxic waste. These toxins are then either eliminated with efficiency, or they are carried off to other parts of our body where they can wreak havoc in various ways.

Sluggish or constipated bowels can result in autointoxication, a process where the body literally poisons itself on its own toxic juices. These toxins from the colon are reabsorbed into the bloodstream and carried to every cell in our body. This is how autointoxication can be the root cause of many of today's diseases and illnesses. Such conditions as arthritis, rheumatism, inflammation and many other undesirable symptoms can result in serious discomfort and poor health.

When the body gets a build-up of toxins that it has difficulty handling with efficiency and effectiveness, it usually presents itself in the form of skin eruptions, or in the form of illness and disease. Usually, we can trace this back to our dietary and lifestyle choices. When these factors are combined with the stress levels of daily living, our system may rebel.

It depends on who or what, a person wants to believe, but the disease is the beginning of the cure. We think that the diarrhoea we got today was because of what we ate yesterday, or that the flu we had last week was because we caught some bug. This may or may not be the case. Possibly, our bodies had been storing these excess toxins and then became overloaded, and eventually rebelled in the form of diarrhoea, flu or some other obvious symptoms.

In all probability, we had been manifesting these outcomes through our daily choices in the three or four weeks prior to the body breaking down. It is entirely possible that we had been manifesting health problems for months, or even years, before visible signs and symptoms appeared. This expression by our body forces us to take care of ourselves and is an opportunity to begin the healing process. Most people have difficulty with this perspective and we often make the recovery process more difficult for ourselves as a result.

We do this by taking all kinds of remedies that may impede the body's need and ability to eliminate these stored up toxins. The body's natural immunity is an amazing mechanism that is capable of doing wonderful things on our behalf, particularly if we help it. Our responsibility is to appreciate this and take care of it, just like we would some precious material possession, only this is more important.

It is becoming more common for people to augment their natural elimination processes with other fashionable and sometimes, effective cleansing processes. Processes such as fasting and colon hydrotherapy (colonics) are becoming increasingly popular as methods to assist in the elimination of toxins from the human body. Fasting is relatively common and has taken place for centuries.

There are various types of fasting processes that can be useful in the elimination of toxins from the body and some of these fasting diets claim to work effectively on specific body organs. A good friend of mine has fasted several times and recommends using "The Master Cleanser" by Stanley Burroughs. The Master Cleanser is often referred to as the "Lemonade Diet" and is published by Burroughs Books, which is located in Auburn, California.

The reasons for fasting in olden times were many, including both religious and cultural. By comparison, colonics are relatively new. They are gaining in popularity, as a means of manually eliminating toxins from the body by working with the colon. The procedure is commonly referred to as colon cleansing. It is a procedure that is similar in technique to having an enema, but is a more gentle process, and it involves less strain and stress for the individual involved. Colon hydrotherapy is one of the most direct ways to effectively cleanse the colon of imbedded fecal plaque, helping to cleanse and restore the colon to a healthy functioning state.

It is worth remembering that the efficient elimination of waste from our system is extremely important to living a healthy, happy and prosperous life. I cannot overstate this. Now I am so regular that the uncomfortable past is only a reminder of how fortunate I am that I discovered life beyond laxatives!

Sleep

"I can wake up at 9 A.M. and be rested or I can wake up at 6 A.M. and be President."

—Jimmy Carter

We are probably on occasion all guilty of not getting enough sleep. I have several friends who don't seem to sleep at all. I have other friends who seem to sleep away the best hours of their lives. Why is this?

Although we humans seem to possess the same nervous system, we all have a different biochemistry. There are so many factors that influence our biochemistry and, for this reason, different people need varying amounts of sleep and rest depending on their personal makeup and circumstance. Our personal makeup and circumstances can be affected by our level of activity, oxygen consumption, lifestyle, diet, stress levels, relationships and generally where we are at a particular point in time.

Most people underestimate the importance of adequate amounts of sleep. Cheating on our sleep can and does compromise our immune system, sometimes with major consequences. When I catch a cold or some other respiratory ailment, it can usually be traced to lack of rest and sleep. Yes, I am attempting to correct my hypocritical ways by taking my own best advice and being sensitive to my need for extra rest when my immune system is under attack. I can truthfully say that my ability to recover from respiratory setback is directly related to the amount of rest and sleep that I give my body.

The issue of getting enough sleep is even more relevant because of the fast-paced society in which we live and the stress that competition can impose on us. The consequences of not getting enough sleep can result in unnecessary accidents, mistakes and loss of temper. It doesn't stop there because our actions and indiscretions often impact other people, sometimes resulting in irreversible damage.

Sleep disorders are a growing and challenging health problem. A good friend of mine who used to be the department head for respiratory therapy at the Aberhart, as a natural progression of her work, branched out into the field of sleep study. She was one of the first professionals in North America to go into this important area of work. She took her skills and talents from the Aberhart in Edmonton, Alberta, to Winnipeg, Manitoba, and then to Las Vegas, Nevada, where she opened two sleep study labs. Our lack of sleep ensures that she will have no shortage of clients.

We all need to understand the importance of getting both enough sleep and rest in order that we give ourselves the best chance to remain both active and healthy.

A SIMPLE TOOL—"WISER"

A frustration that I have often experienced when taking courses or advice is not that the information isn't useful, but rather that I am left to my own devices as to how to apply it to my life. It seems that information is one thing, applying it is another. It's easy to tell people that they should eat a healthy diet, get more exercise and eat less fat, but the question is, why don't more people do it? The answer is, they don't have the proper motivation for doing it. When people have good reasons to do things, it becomes easier for them to do whatever is required. It means that the incentive for the modification of their personal behaviour has been established.

If you are a person who finds it difficult to change and you are reluctant to follow complicated or conflicting advice that you have received, then try to remember the word "WISER."

It stands for five principles:

1. "W" stands for water—drink lots of it.
2. "I" stands for inhale deeply several times a day.
3. "S" stands for slow down and chew your food longer.
4. "E" stands for exercise your body and/or your mind.
5. "R" stands for rest and sleep—it's vitally important.

If this is all you learn and all you remember from reading this book, I can guarantee that your life will be enhanced through better health.

Intangibles *of* Health

PURPOSE IN LIFE

"It is my observation that more people are expressing a desire for something that will give meaning to their lives."
—Theodor Klassen PhD in his booklet
Perspectives on the Transformational Power of Love

Why don't people, take better care of themselves? On the surface it would seem like such a natural thing to do, and yet most of us fail on this account. This is a perplexing question, especially if we know what to do and still we don't do it. I know, because at times I am as guilty as the next person.

I have studied personal growth technologies in depth and, as a result, have come to the conclusion that most people don't do things in life because they don't have a big enough reason. It usually boils down to people knowing what they don't want and not what they do want. In other words, very few people have a purpose in life. If we have a purpose in life we have all the reason we need to motivate ourselves and move forward with enthusiasm and focus. The purpose doesn't have to be anything more than a direction and usually it involves other people.

My observation in the area of personal health is similar to the field of personal growth. That observation is that people usually wait until they have a big enough reason before they will begin to take better care of themselves. We have all heard personal declarations such as, "I will quit next week" or some other reference to addressing personal change that has health implications.

Because of my experience in hospital I saw the end stages of many unfortunate circumstances that resulted from people either not taking care of themselves, or not knowing how or what to do. It seems that an inordinate number of us wait until we have a heart attack, get cancer, diabetes or some other condition before we get the message. Human beings are supposed to be smarter than that, but apparently we aren't.

There was an article in the newspaper that pointed out that baby boomers were fat and fifty, which in all likelihood will result in increased health care requirements in the not too distant future. The reasons included the fact that we boomers have eaten high fat diets for too long and that for a large number of us our cholesterol levels are beyond recommended levels. Our dietary sins appear to be catching up to us.

About the same time as that news story occurred, the Canadian government was warning the public that the Canada Pension Plan was going to be in trouble, because there wasn't going to be enough people working to support the aging boomers. This was the alarm telling Canadians that they would need to contribute more to the Plan or it would not be sustained. The next day there was a cartoon on the editorial page showing the Prime Minister telling everyone to relax, because most boomers wouldn't live long enough to be able to collect from the Canadian Pension Plan anyway! This is a sad indictment of our lifestyle choices and of our ability to apply knowledge.

Granted, having a heart attack or getting cancer can be the personal motivation an individual may need to begin to look after themselves, but surely, there must be a better way. We, as intelligent people, need to create motivational reasons for taking care of ourselves long before getting into health difficulties. I know this may be easier said than done, but if we don't have an obvious purpose in life then maybe it is time that we gave of ourselves to other people. That is why volunteerism can be so powerful and meaningful for those who help others.

At this point I would like to share some information and words of wisdom from a woman who embodies the idea of unconditionally giving.

Margaret Cammaert dedicated her life to the improvement of nursing and health services for the poor and oppressed in third world countries, particularly Latin America and the Caribbean. In recognition of her work she was awarded an Honorary Doctor of Laws Degree from the University of Alberta.

In her address to the graduating students she said that to know and keep in touch with the meaning of her life was vitally important in both her career and in her life. It not only gave direction, and shaped who she became, but also was a powerful motivator, and strengthened her in times of adversity. Like most young adults, when she left the University the meaning of her life was focused on external objects such as building a successful career, financial security and adventure. It was only when she became older and had more or less attained her external goals, that she then began the journey inwards to explore that vast inner world that is unique to each one of us. She says it is here that we find a different meaning of our life and who we really are. Unless we make the inner journey, we risk spending the latter years of our life with a stranger, someone we never took the time to meet.

It has been proven that people will do more for others than they will usually do for themselves. Think about that statement and ask yourself if that was, or is, true in your case and for the people in your immediate circle of family and friends. Ask yourself when you felt the happiest and most loved in your life. It was probably when you were giving of yourself to others, whether you knew them or not. W. Clement Stone was one of the first people to study positive mental attitudes. He once said, "If you give unconditionally, it is almost impossible to give more than you receive."

In my case, I have several built-in reasons to take care of myself, namely in the form of my beautiful wife, Valerie, and my lovely children, Keiko and Jamie, who have taught me so much about life. The youthful enthusiasm that they impart is a tonic that has beneficial health effects for me. They have reinforced for me just how important it is to relate to one another in an honest, open and trusting way.

Now I realize more than ever how much damage can be done by things that I say or do, or conversely, how powerful a supportive comment and word of encouragement can be in the development and lives of others, especially my children. Whether we realize it or not, as adults our every word and action is being measured by some young mind.

Words are extremely powerful and I think the late Norman Cousins was accurate when he said "Words can kill"; conversely, I believe that words of encouragement, support, warmth and caring can be critical to both the healing process and good health. Sometimes we say things that can be just what another person needs to hear at that moment in time. This is particularly true if we are cognizant of the fact of how important words are.

Often it is not only what we say, but how we say it. This is borne out by the research that says thirty-eight per cent of communication is voice tonality. That same study said that fifty-five per cent of communication is how we use our physiology (body language) in expressing ourselves. This is very important because sincerity of expression is contained in how we say something, which can be as important as what we say. A paraphrase of the old schoolyard saying could be, "Sticks and stones can break my bones but words can kill me."

When it comes to health and healing, we often wait for some medical opinion to tell us how we feel and what the long-term prognosis is for our particular condition. If, at this point, we have a condition that is chronic or in deterioration, we will more than likely respond in accordance with the medical opinion which is such a powerful influence. Most medical opinions are based on both statistics and conjecture. The problem with statistics is that they are often a result of studying sick people and what is normal or the average for sick people is not necessarily applicable to individuals in specific cases. I have seen people give up hope on the words of some respected authority figure and, conversely, I have seen people respond in somewhat of a miraculous manner, catalyzed by what they have been told. Ultimately, our health and healing ability is up to us and to our mind, body, soul and spirit.

Labels that are used to describe situations and conditions give a context and parameters so that we can make determinations and prescribe accordingly. This can be useful to those who are diagnosing and prescribing remedies. The same labels can, however, be poison to the individual who has been labelled. Swedish theologian Soren Kierkegaard once said, "When you label me you negate me."

In other words, if we have been told that we have cancer or some other condition that conjures up all kinds of internal fears, and we are told that we have six months to live and we believe it, then that's what we have. This may be an oversimplification, but the point is, that statistics provide only one piece of information. It does not take into account the things that can be changed such as lifestyle, or the love, caring and connection that may be available to that person who has the diagnosis. It also does not take into account a person's personal, religious and spiritual beliefs, nor does it take into consideration beliefs about their own potential. One of the biggest things to take into consideration is that person's reason for living, or in other words, purpose in life.

In his book, *Seven Spiritual Laws of Success*, Dr. Deepak Chopra writes that if there is one thing he could influence in the lives of his children, it would be for them to establish a purpose in life. This would give them a reason for being and ultimately give life its meaning. Beginning to understand what he meant has been very important for me as I move forward in my own life.

This chapter in his book has also made me realize that this is extremely important to not only my health, but to the health of others. After becoming aware of this I went back into my past and looked at my personal and spiritual development and its impact on my health. I realized that when I was growing in both areas it was because I had big enough reasons. Whether it was in the area of relationships, volunteerism, career or whatever, it was all directly related to doing something meaningful in my life at that particular time.

Our reasons for being and doing can and will change throughout our lifetime. Our purpose in life may also change or it may be a lifelong calling. The purpose in life can be discovered early or later, such as with Mother Teresa. The important thing about reasons and purpose is that they are like a magnet that pulls us forward in life with meaning, a sense of self-worth and the satisfaction of knowing that we are making a positive contribution to ourselves and others. Remember people will often do more for others (including their pets!) than they will for themselves.

In summation, purpose gives our lives meaning and meaning gives us a reason for living. And reasons for living mean that we need to be healthy in body, mind and spirit, which gives us the psychological and emotional nourishment that we need to take care of ourselves. It is only when we take care of ourselves that we can be healthy and contribute in a meaningful way. Most of us wander, without a compass, in what is tantamount to an emotional and spiritual wilderness. A purpose in life will provide us with the compass we need to find our emotional and spiritual way.

HOPE

Hope is what keeps most of us going, particularly in times of difficulty and when we are discouraged. Without it most of us would give up and become self-destructive or maybe even express ourselves in a manner of civil disobedience and violence. As a society it is imperative that we never let our members down so far that they give up in despair. It all begins and ends at the level of the individual. We can plant the seeds of hope and nurture them or we can sow the seeds of despair and watch ourselves deteriorate in ruin.

Without a purpose in life we will wander aimlessly, but without hope people will just give up and often become unpredictable and irrational. Often, people who are trapped in a cycle of poverty with no apparent way out will turn to alcohol and drugs, or some other form of self-destructive behaviour. A feeling of hopelessness can overwhelm people and lead them to a desire to put an end to it all.

It is up to all of us to support one another with both kind words and deeds. The positive return for us, as individuals and as communities, are incalculable, just as the negative results would be.

Hope is often expressed through individual dreams and we should never pour cold water on anyone's dreams. Remember that if we have achieved any of our goals or dreams it is probably because someone believed in us and supported us when we needed it most.

In August 1997 Wallace Immen, medical reporter for the *Globe and Mail* newspaper, wrote a column on "How hope can beat the odds against illness." He asked the question: Can a doctor cure a person who doesn't want to get better? In the article he quoted several notable researchers and gave various bits of anecdotal information after which he stated: "Without an underlying belief that things will get better, the mind tends to focus on the negative, and these mental images can create physical effects." Essentially the answer to his original question is "No."

In my own case, my mother tells the story of when I first got polio and how I had been given hope, in the form of a dog. My parents knew that I loved animals and that I was particularly fond of dogs. They told me that if I recovered and became well again, they would buy me a Sealyham terrier. When I first entered the hospital, I was in and out of consciousness. This is why I only vaguely recall the whole experience. The point is that this hope in the form of a dog is what may have saved my life.

We have all heard the saying "Hope springs eternal," and it reminds me of a quote from a friend of mine named Christine. She wrote: "From yesterday's thoughts come today's seeds that will blossom into tomorrow's flowers."

EMOTIONAL NEEDS

When I used to think about my health and taking care of myself, I mainly thought of exercise, diet and drinking water. In practice, I attempted to limit the use of potentially harmful substances such as alcohol, but nevertheless enjoying a drink or more on occasion. It really never occurred to me that there were other elements that could be as important to my health. In fact, I now realize that the obvious areas of exercise and diet are only a piece of a much more complex puzzle called our health.

Gwen Randall-Young, a chartered psychologist and the author of *Dancing Soul*, refers to "emotional malnutrition." Emotional malnutrition is when we experience a lack of nourishment for the emotional, psychological and spiritual elements of our being. This lack of emotional nourishment can manifest itself in many ways, including depression, and can also affect our physical body through a variety of medical conditions. Medications may alleviate the symptoms but will not do anything to address the underlying causes of those symptoms. Ultimately, the responsibility for healing the wounds of the past is ours.

Often true healing cannot occur until we nourish our emotional selves. The evidence from psychological research confirms that we can go into the emotional history of our being and retroactively heal ourselves through imagery, forgiveness and love. This is important to know even if it may be difficult to do. Virtually everything we think, do, say, touch, feel and experience can and will affect our health, either in the short term or the long term. Basically, as we interact with our environment, others and ourselves, there is a consequence. How we internalize and metabolize this interaction will ultimately determine our quality of life and our quality of health.

We must continually nourish our emotional and spiritual needs in order to experience true health. Ultimately, it is up to each one of us to determine how we feel. In other words whatever happens to us, whether it be internal and within our control, or external and beyond our control, we do have the ability to interpret the event or situation and give it a personal meaning. It is this personal meaning that will affect our emotions and how we move forward from there.

I am sure we have all seen a situation where two people have come through the same experience, whether it is a trauma or what might be considered a joyous occasion, and come out of it with completely opposite perspectives or interpretations. In most cases, this is great in the sense that it gives us our individuality and sometimes develops our personality. On other occasions these perspectives and interpretations can be a destructive or disruptive force in our lives.

I learned a long time ago that one of the most important influences in my life was how I talked to myself, either in words or thoughts. This was one of the biggest revelations in my life. In my view, nourishing our emotional needs begins with how we talk to ourselves (self-talk or inner dialogue). Just listen to the people around you and listen to yourself, and you will soon get an understanding of what I mean. Many people in this world go around saying all kinds of negative things to themselves and do not realize that they are continually reinforcing negative emotions. These negative emotions can, and no doubt will, be a contributing factor to whatever goes on in their life, including impacting their personal health.

Our thoughts and emotions are the main keys to our personal "drug store" within our bodies. It is this apothecary that generates the biochemicals our body needs in the form of Valium, bacterial fighting substances and whatever else we may need at the time. Our body makes every drug we need and is capable of making them in the exact quantities we require to handle virtually every situation. If we talk to ourselves, think positive thoughts and visualize constructively, our body will respond by sending a wave of nourishing biochemicals throughout our system. Conversely, our body is equally as capable of sending poisonous toxins throughout our system, which can have very negative and damaging consequences on our emotional and physical health.

I have only touched on a very complex area, which is all part of the ongoing research into the mind, body, soul and spirit approaches to healing. There are theories that say emotions and experiences of our relatives can be passed from generation to generation through our genetic makeup. This is difficult for straightforward thinkers like me, but I happen to believe that anything is possible in this universe and that humankind (me included) still has much to learn. We have a tendency as a populace to make everything as black and white as possible in order to enhance our understanding, and the area of healing or medicine is no different in this respect.

The reason I mention this is because often we cannot fathom why someone would get cancer, multiple sclerosis or some other illness or disease that is often traced back to lifestyle habits, when on the surface they appeared to have done everything according to the book. There are some things that cannot be explained in language that we understand. Maybe these individuals of whom I speak are not only dealing with the consequences of their lifestyle choices, but they may also be dealing with factors that have been passed through DNA from one generation to another. We can say "hogwash" or "bunk" to this type of thinking, but I would not dismiss it so quickly. Life is complex and all I know is the more I learn the less I seem to know.

Factors such as genetics, pre-disposition to particular conditions and other elements that might be beyond our control, are things that we all have to accommodate in our lives. This does not change those things that are within our control, things such as our inner dialogue. It pains me to see people, including many of my good friends, constantly beat themselves up emotionally without realizing what they are actually doing to themselves.

Worse yet, it doesn't stop there. These individuals reinforce these internal negative emotions generated by self-talk and then interact with others, sometimes with unfortunate results. This ripple effect can carry over and strain relationships and other people's feelings towards us. The reason this is important to know is that we nourish ourselves emotionally through our inner dialogue, our actions and through our relationships with others. It is also important to be aware of the fact that our external world is usually a direct mirror of these thoughts and actions. This is a perspective that is well understood by anyone who has studied personal growth, psychology and theory, and its practical application and effect.

If you want friends, you first have to be a friend. If you want love, you first have to give love. And if you want other people to care about you, you first must care about others. So often in life people fail to grasp this lesson and it is one that I am guilty of forgetting on occasion. Every once in a while I need to pull myself back into line by taking a look at the results I'm getting in a given situation or in a given relationship by asking the question, "What am I doing in my approach to generate this response?" This will often steer me back on course and assist me in maintaining an emotional balance.

There are people more eloquent than me, who have expounded on emotions and relationships. However, the one thing I do know and can say with conviction is that nourishing our emotional needs can be as important to our health, and in some cases more important, than whether we ate junk food yesterday or failed to exercise. Emotions can have a life-long consequence and we should not dismiss them offhandedly or make light of what someone else is dealing with. It is our responsibility to be supportive of others, but we can only do this if we first nourish ourselves, which all begins with what we say to ourselves and what we think.

I have talked about our emotional health as individuals, but the health of the society we live in is also a direct reflection of how we, as a collection of individuals, relate to others. To illustrate this point I want to share with you something that I wrote about after a particular emotional debate that took place around the subject of discrimination in Alberta. What are beliefs and where do they come from? What about biases and prejudices? What is hatred and racism and where do they come from? Why do certain people make us uncomfortable? Is there anything that we can do personally to change any of the attitudes that we have? If so, what can we do?

These questions and more came to mind as I listened to the emotional debate that Albertans were having. It forced me to reflect on my own personal experience when I was growing up in the University Hospital in Edmonton. Some of the experiences that I replayed in my mind brought back a realization that at one time I was inclined to prejudice and racism. It was a time in my life when I was naive, ignorant and somewhat fearful of what I didn't know. I am ashamed of the unwarranted prejudicial attitudes that I held. However, I am proud to say that I have grown beyond this prejudicial and fearful mindset. I am now a richer man because I have learned, where before I deprived myself of many of life's riches because of my prevailing negative attitudes.

I lived on the polio ward and was completely dependent on the staff and volunteers for my every physical need. We had a predominantly white staff made up of English-speaking workers. Many of them were immigrants from various European countries. Over time the complexion of the workforce on the polio ward began to change. There was a sprinkling of various nationalities that began to change the staff mix. As long as I had someone that was taking care of me who was white and English speaking, I felt comfortable. The minute that I was put in a position of being cared for by someone with dark skin I remember becoming uncomfortable. However, I never knew why until I began to confront my biases, prejudices and fears.

I gradually began to confront my feelings and deal with them in a rational way. I also had some additional leverage because I realized I was not in a strong position to enforce my ignorant beliefs. When a person has the choice of laying in bed without service because of prejudice, or a choice of being respectful and tolerant, the choice becomes somewhat easier. When I began to see and understand that these angels of colour from different cultures were kind, caring and compassionate people, I began to change my beliefs about others.

I also wonder where these prejudices that I was feeling came from. The only things that I could remember were quick little glimpses of things my father and others that I was around would say. I remember my dad saying such things as, "That new Chinaman who runs the corner store seems like a decent enough fella!" The inference was that somehow this was a surprise to him. There were also many other influences through other people's biases, including my roommates and the staff. I am also sure that I picked up some of my prejudices in the schoolyard and in the community that I grew up in. The Indian residential school was just a few kilometres down the road from where we lived in the Yukon Territory. I also remember the jokes and humour being somewhat vicious when I think about it.

I am pleased to say that many of these people from varying cultures have become very close friends. Not only that, they have enriched my life in so many ways that I can only begin to express my appreciation and thanks to, and love, for them. If I had remained in my old prejudicial mindset I would have denied myself, my family and my God.

People might say that this is different from confronting beliefs about homosexuality. Maybe, maybe not. A very close friend that was a key mentor in my life turned out to be gay. I didn't know this initially, and therefore, I was able to see my friend as a person who I admired deeply. When I found out that he was gay I had to deal with those feelings. Ultimately, I was able to realize that nothing had changed except that I had a deeper understanding of the man. He was the same guy and the choice was mine as to whether our relationship would be any different. I owe him a great deal because he helped shape my development and made me a better person. I will always be grateful to him for what he has given me.

This experience with my friend gave me a different perspective on homosexuality. Since then I have realized that they are the same as you and me.

Remember the words of a great man when he said: "Do unto others as you would have them do unto you"; and "Love thy neighbour as thy self."

The social challenges that we have in society can be traced to how we respond emotionally and how that emotion translates into actions of love, hatred, vindictiveness or caring. It has often been said that we can get a glimpse into the health of a society by the way that society treats those that are disadvantaged in some way. The health of a society is built on how we care for and relate to one another, because that's where it all starts. So if you and I, and we as a collective, want to have good emotional health, we must take a good look at how we treat others and whether we respect, appreciate, love and truly care for them. This is where emotional health begins and ends.

HUMOUR—ITS IMPORTANCE

"Methuselah ate what he found on his plate, and never, as people do now, did he note the amount of the calorie count; he ate it because it was chow. He wasn't disturbed as at a dinner he sat, devouring a roast or a pie, to think it was lacking in the right kind of fat or a couple of vitamins shy. He cheerfully chewed each species of food, unmindful of troubles or fears lest his health might be hurt by some fancy dessert, and he lived over nine hundred years!"

—Author Unknown

We hear all the time that we should live a healthy lifestyle by being physically active and practising proper dietary habits. Then we think of people we know who don't seem to do any of the prescribed or recommended approaches for a long and healthy life, yet seem to live to an old age anyway. We may even take this example and use it as a reason or excuse for not modifying our lifestyle, even though we know it may be better than the way we currently conduct ourselves.

It seems to me that even though diet, physical activity, fluid intake and sleep are all very important, there are other factors that can be almost as important and for some people maybe even more important. Maybe these people who appear to do things wrong on the surface have their lives in order in other ways. Just maybe they laugh a lot, maybe they have loving relationships, maybe they love their work and co-workers, or maybe they are just high on life. Humour and good nature can be the fuel we need for healthy emotions and can get us through many difficult and dark times in our lives. I believe some people are naturally gifted with these qualities, but I also believe that these qualities can be cultivated and nurtured if we take the time.

"If you want to live a long time you have to smoke cigars, drink martinis and dance close."

—George Burns

Where I grew up a sense of humour was almost a necessity for survival and certainly for getting along with others. The study of humour can be very revealing in that it often makes light of some very serious situations, concerns and events in our lives. This was certainly the case on the polio ward, as we often coped with a very serious situation by finding the humour in it. It was probably both a coping and survival method and often became a game of one-upmanship between my roommates and me.

We would often get each other laughing so hard that it became difficult to breathe, but overall it was so good for our well-being. There is nothing as basic or crass as institutional humour and particularly in a hospital setting. I think this is because virtually every anatomical part is on display in a variety of situations and this gives rise to some great opportunities for one-liners, and there were many of them. I am only sorry that I didn't write them down because a guy could have made a living doing comedy with all of these lines and stories.

Humour in the work place has become big business as it has been recognized for its importance in developing and maintaining good staff morale. Obviously if the staff are in a good frame of mind it has got to be good for business. Even though we weren't a business per se, the theory and practice of the importance of humour still applied. This was certainly my experience in living in the hospital for those many years.

Studies have conclusively proven that humour actually assists in the healing process. Humour is now being used in therapeutic settings with a variety of illnesses and diseases, most notably with individuals confronted by cancer.

Humour, laughter and good nature are synonymous with health and happiness. Unfortunately we sometimes forget this and all too often we take life too seriously, which can result in unnecessary stress and having to handle the negative fallout from this factor in our lives.

FEAR

"Love and Fear is all there is."

—A Course in Miracles

True paralysis occurs when we are afraid. Fear prevents us from doing things, approaching people, confronting our feelings, flying, taking risks and trying new things. It even enters and affects our most intimate relationships. We may be afraid to make commitments because of a variety of unknown reasons, such as getting hurt or losing something that we don't even have.

In my life I have dealt with physical paralysis, but the only times I have been truly paralyzed and limited have been when I was afraid to try new things, take risks or generally to go beyond my comfort zone and the security of a particular mindset that I held. Virtually every time that I have extended myself physically, emotionally and psychologically, I have benefited more than I could ever imagine. Certainly it was scary. But now I can look back and draw on those references using them to propel and encourage me, as I go through my life when I am confronted with other difficult circumstances. I am sure this is something that we all experience in some way.

Fear of failure is something that most of us have. Why? Where does this come from? What is failure? Is there such a thing? I don't think so. Fear is a perception or an illusion, which is merely an interpretation of our imagination, an experience, a happening or an event. Failure may be a judgment of ourselves or others, which we label as "failure." I think, in the process we are probably not being fair to ourselves or to other people when judging actions or people as failures.

I think that what we often term as a failure is really a lesson in disguise and something that we need to experience in order to learn. Many great accomplishments, inventions and personal turn-a-rounds in life have come from what we would normally perceive as failures.

It may sound silly but there are a great number of people in this world who are afraid of success, and as a consequence, they are held back because of an unknown fear. This has been somewhat difficult for me to understand because it seems that we all want to be successful in some way, and yet we often undermine ourselves, thus preventing success.

What is success, anyway? I remember being asked to give a talk to a group of Grade 5 and 6 students on "success." I was really not sure how to approach this subject and make it meaningful. Fortunately, it turned out to be one of my better presentations and the focus I took was asking the children if they thought there was such a thing as success or such a thing as failure. After a variety of answers, I said I don't think there is any such thing as a failure and I gave them some examples based on the feedback they had just given me. What one child termed a failure, another termed it a success. For example, if one child brought home a mark of seventy per cent in math, that was a success. To another, it was a failure.

I talked about there being no failures, only lessons. And I then asked them what they thought would happen in their life if they went through it with this approach.

When we have no choice, like being forced to deal with a traumatic accident, an illness, marriage break-up or some other difficult circumstance, we somehow manage to draw on resources we didn't know we had. It has been said that we only use ten to fifteen per cent of our brain, and I think this is also true for most of us when it comes to tapping our personal human resources and potential to deal with life's challenges and opportunities.

When we are dealt these cards of difficulty, we are thrust into an unknown and foreign situation and are forced to deal with it. Some people can rise to the occasion and actually come out of it better than they were before they were confronted. Others will give up and die either literally, or emotionally.

One of the greatest fears that people have is to become disabled through illness and disease or by experiencing an accident. They may harbour these fears and express them through their attitudes and biases towards other people, who may actually be living with the feared condition or circumstance. This can translate into what we think of, and how we act towards, others who are less fortunate than ourselves. I think all of us at our deepest level are basically kind and caring individuals. But sometimes we get away from this and as a result our attitude towards others can become hardened and callused.

These hardened attitudes come with their costs to our health. I say this because if we are basically kind, caring and compassionate people, and yet we project an attitude of being pious, or generally one that is incongruent with who we really are, then we are in conflict with ourselves. When we are in conflict with ourselves we have this internal emotional struggle which may continually surface in the form of negative emotions. These negative emotions may be expressed in the form of fear, which in turn can lead to a deterioration of our health whether it, be physically, psychologically, emotionally or spiritually.

The best medicine for fear, particularly if we have a choice, is to confront it head on. The reason is that once you do something or go through an experience there is no need to be afraid of it any longer. I am reminded of some events in my forty-eighth year, when I was taking some Anthony Robbins' courses. I was in this weekend seminar where everybody was doing a board-breaking exercise, which was a metaphor for breaking through your most dominant fear(s). I made all kinds of excuses to myself as to why I shouldn't attempt to break the board. Excuses like I might break my foot (because my foot was the most logical part of me to use to break the board) and, as a result, I didn't do it. However, there was a little voice in the back of my head that was telling me that I should do it and that really I was just chicken and fabricating excuses. I kept justifying it with thinking I was physically disabled and that if I broke my foot as a result of this foolish (for me) metaphorical experience, that it would have negative consequences and would affect my family, my job, blah blah blah!

In the summer of 1994 my wife and I along with several friends attended the "Life Mastery" portion of Anthony Robbins' Mastery University. This ten-day experience was one of the most phenomenal and fun times of my life. It could be termed the ultimate children's camp for adults and is an experience that I wish everyone could have. I not only met wonderful people from all over the world but I learned and gained some valuable insights into life and into myself.

While I was there I did a modified version of a firewalk on hot coals. Initially I wasn't going to attempt to do it, but then I justified doing it by thinking the worst thing that could happen would be that I would burn my foot, and I could always stop before doing any major damage. It was for this reason that I decided to go ahead and do it, knowing it was a situation where all I needed to do was get myself into that mental state through the power of focus and belief.

It was easy to come to this conclusion because many people had done the firewalk before me and not had any negative consequences. And I knew that I was certainly capable of controlling my focus and belief system. In case you are wondering how I did it, Tony Robbins pushed my wheelchair alongside the bed of hot coals and I put my bare left foot in the coals, mimicking what would be considered steps for others. I must say this was a very liberating experience in the sense that it had been some time since I had challenged myself physically.

I learned several lessons from that experience and I did go back to Edmonton where I broke the board with my foot not only once, but on three different occasions. On the third occasion I probably learned more because I had great difficulty in going through the board, whereas the first two times were quite easy by comparison. One of the things I learned on the third occasion was that it is not necessarily what you do that is the most important thing, but rather what you learn and how you apply those lessons. The lessons for me were facing my fear head on, and the importance of perseverance in the face of these fears.

We can all learn from children in the sense that children seldom give up and will continue in the face of almost insurmountable odds. This occurs when they are learning to walk, ride a bicycle or some other activity where they may experience falling. They may get hurt or bruised as a result of taking risks and learning through experience, but they stay determined. Their natural instincts are to pick themselves up, dust themselves off and keep going until they have mastered the task at hand. Every time I watch my children learn something new through taking risks, I learn. I often wonder what life would be like if we could recapture the passion, intensity, spirit and enthusiasm that we had as children, and that we were born with. Somehow I think most of us would be healthier and more fun to be around if this were the case.

FAITH

If love is the antidote for hate then faith is the antidote for fear. It has been described by some as the ultimate resource that we have at our disposal. Faith plays a part in our lives every day, although we may not realize it. If we didn't have faith, we wouldn't be able to drive down a two-lane highway where we are only separated from other cars by a thin white or yellow line. Without a form of faith we would be reluctant to cross a street, go out of our house and we certainly wouldn't trust anyone or anything.

Faith can be applied to many situations, but where it can be most effective is in dealing with the unknown or the uncommon occurrence that we may be faced with in life. Think about it, if you don't have faith it is very difficult if not impossible to be effective, let alone be happy and healthy. Faith is most often equated with religion, which is probably appropriate in the sense that the biggest questions we have about life revolve around our existence, the meaning of life, our purpose on this earth and our relationship with our Creator. No one can be sure in concrete terms, but what we can all have is faith, if we so choose.

It is always useful to have an expected outcome when going places, doing things or even meeting people. My outcome for my "Life Mastery" experience was to become more spiritually connected. I was fortunate to have accomplished this in the first two days of this powerful life experience. During the ten-day course there were many great and well-known presenters. The two that had an impact for me in the area of faith and spirituality were Captain Gerald Coffey and Dr. Deepak Chopra.

Captain Coffey was a prisoner during the Vietnam War and spent seven years in solitary confinement with virtually no verbal contact with anyone or the outside world. His explanation and feelings about what most of us would perceive as Hell on Earth were extremely important for me. In fact, what he had to say was just what I needed to hear at that point in my life.

He spoke about faith and the importance of it and some of the forms it comes in. I specifically remember him saying how important it was for him, and something that should be equally as important for you and me. He was referring to four different faiths that pulled him through this ordeal: faith in his country, faith in his fellow man, faith in himself and, above all, faith in his God.

Dr. Chopra spoke about a subject that he has become known for, his understanding of the universal intelligence and our personal relationship with it. He took what I consider to be a most complex subject and explained it in very understandable terms. Even in understandable terms, it is still something I continually need to go over in order to grasp the significance of his intellect, insights and wisdom.

His explanations were shared with the audience between 12 A.M. and 2:30 A.M. and I noticed several people nodding off, but not me. I was able to stay awake for two reasons, one being that I was totally absorbed by what he was saying and the second reason being that I didn't have my respirator to help me breathe, so it was impossible for me to fall asleep!

The practical application of faith that was shared by Captain Gerald Coffey and the insightful explanations provided by Dr. Deepak Chopra gave me a much deeper understanding of life, the universe and my place in it. This in turn has combined with my own interpretations and previous understanding to give me a more complete faith in this area of my life. It was also interesting for me to hear that Captain Coffey wouldn't exchange this experience in his life for anything because of what he learned about himself, life, his country and his God.

Faith has an important role in our health because it is so powerful in overcoming and combating our fears.

There have been studies done and books written about the power of prayer and its effect on assisting the healing process in overcoming illness and disease. Faith works in concert with our belief systems, our subconscious mind and with the universal intelligence on our behalf.

Without faith it is not possible to be happy and healthy. With faith virtually anything is possible. There are many examples of seemingly impossible situations being reversed and termed miracles because the results defy logic and are beyond explanation. If you look closely at a creative invention, major discovery or the conquering of illness, disease or Mt. Everest, you will find that an unshakeable faith was behind it. It is faith that can be our guide throughout our lives if we choose to draw on it.

Observations have been made that are supported by studies that show people who have a strong faith are healthier and live longer than those who don't. These individuals of whom I speak, have a strong faith in themselves and in their Creator. They also have a meaningful purpose in life, which makes them feel wanted and useful.

BELIEF SYSTEMS

Our belief system is very powerful in dictating what goes on in our lives and is responsible for the actions we take on a daily basis. The connection between what we believe and our faith that I described earlier, combine to form a potent resource which can have a dramatic affect on virtually every aspect of our life.

Faith is a feeling and a belief in a power greater than any one of us. It is a type of belief and is a resource that we can always draw on, whereas beliefs are generally shaped by what we are taught both directly and indirectly, as well as what we experience throughout a lifetime, beginning at birth.

Our biases and prejudices towards someone or something are simply beliefs that have been formed over time. Sometimes we come to these beliefs based on our own experience. At other times we may have formulated a bias or prejudice through the influence of other people's beliefs. Beliefs can and do change over time and often are a measure of our personal growth in a given aspect of our lives.

Dr. Maxwell Maltz, who is both a physician and writer, regularly shares the following story with his audiences to illustrate the power of negative beliefs and how we can change them.

> Psychiatrist Alfred Adler, a student and associate of Sigmund Freud, got off to a bad start learning arithmetic in school. His teacher became convinced that he was poor in mathematics.
>
> One day, however, when the teacher put a problem on the blackboard that no one in the class could do, Adler realized he could work out the answer. When he raised his hand, the teacher and everyone in the class laughed.
>
> Indignant, Adler went to the board and, much to their amazement, worked out the problem. On that day he realized that he could understand arithmetic and that he could become a good math student.
>
> Before this he had been hypnotized by a false belief about himself. The same thing can happen to anyone.

If we have accepted an idea from ourselves, our teachers, parents, friends, advertisements or from any other source, and we are convinced the idea is true, it has the same power over us as a hypnotist can have. We are all hypnotized by our fears and our frustrations because they become a habit. They create a pattern we can't break, just as a hypnotized person can't break the pattern the hypnotist makes that person follow. We carry negative feelings from our job to our home, to our bed and then back to the job. We unnecessarily burden ourselves with extra tensions that make us less than what we are. These negative ideas have exactly the same effect upon our behaviour as the negative ideas implanted into the mind of a hypnotized subject by a professional hypnotist.

How can we de-hypnotize ourselves? Regardless of how big a failure we think we are, we all have the resources within ourselves to change what we believe and to control our subsequent actions. These resources, ability or power becomes available to us just as soon as we can de-hypnotize ourselves from the ideas of "I can't," "I'm not worthy," "I don't deserve it" or other self-limiting thoughts. Think about it, and de-hypnotize yourself from false beliefs.

A simple example would be that when I was about seven years old I thought that girls were sissies and were not nearly as much fun as boys. I certainly didn't understand why someone who was fourteen wanted to have a girlfriend. I would say my beliefs around girls have changed significantly!

My beliefs around food, different cultures and religions, politics, about people, have all changed and evolved over time. The change has occurred as I have become more informed, appreciative, respectful and knowledgeable about a variety of subject matter. My beliefs were and are a direct reflection of my personal growth in any given aspect of my life. They will continue to evolve and change as I continue my journey on this earth. I believe this is true for all people.

Other examples of beliefs are the different religions that exist. Religions are built around a certain dogma or set of beliefs that form the basis for the espoused doctrine. Our inability as humans to tolerate, respect and, most of all, appreciate other people's beliefs and perspectives, is the underpinning of most conflicts. These conflicts create unnecessary sadness, heartache and often inflict undue hardship on others.

A label can be another form of belief. It can be very powerful if internalized and if it becomes part of our own personal identity. This is why labels are so damaging. Let me elaborate. There is no question that I have an obvious physical disability. But I don't see myself as being disabled or handicapped, nor do I see myself as being different from the rest of the population. My actions and outcomes are directly related to my self-image. Self-image is directly related to personal belief systems. That is one of the main reasons that two people can have similar circumstances but entirely different outcomes and experiences.

Beliefs that we all have work together to form a collective community or societal belief. This societal belief is often interpreted as public policy. This public policy, in order to be effective, must also change and evolve over time.

We are now at a major crossroads as regards our personal and collective beliefs about health, public policy and our personal role and responsibility.

Beliefs will dictate the actions we take to eliminate, eradicate and minimize the effects of poverty on health. Socioeconomic status has been shown to be a major determinant in the health of individuals and in the health of communities. We know that health is more than about money, but the way we are currently structured politically, economically and socially, is a reflection of our collective beliefs in this important area. We virtually all agree that change is needed, but it is the actions we take that will determine our outcomes and affect our ability to come to a resolve. Remember, as individuals we have unlimited potential and it is our personal beliefs which determine how much of this potential we can access at any given time. It is beliefs that determine the actions we take on a regular basis and, in turn, it is these actions which will determine our personal and societal outcomes. These outcomes will affect what we believe and will be reflected through increased knowledge, experience and future actions.

The first thing we can do is to become aware of what we believe and to attempt to determine how this is affecting our personal actions. If we are to take responsibility for, and have control of, our personal health, this determination is of paramount importance. Make no mistake about it, what we personally believe will directly affect our ability to maintain, retain and regain our health in the twenty-first century. We do have control over what we believe and where we place our personal and collective emphasis. The question is, are you and I up to the task?

THE SUBCONSCIOUS MIND

I have read several books and attended many seminars and courses on health, goal-setting, positive thinking, motivation and generally on how to design your life to have anything you want. Most of these materials offer sound suggestions and virtually all of them in some way refer to the power of our subconscious mind. Our subconscious mind is where our hidden power is housed. It is also where our connection to the universe and its intelligence takes place.

My research shows and my understanding is that our subconscious mind is programmed by our conscious thoughts. Therefore, the way we think and what we believe has significant impact on our health, both good and bad. With this insight I want to give you a glimpse into this powerful tool that is at our disposal.

Dr. Joseph Murphy wrote an excellent book called *The Power Of Your Subconscious Mind*. He calls your subconscious mind "Your Book of Life." He essentially says that what a person writes on the inside, they will experience on the outside.

From where do we get our inspiration, intuition, guidance and memory? Who, or what, controls our breathing, heartbeat, circulation, digestion, assimilation? Our subconscious mind is always working on our behalf, and I believe that its machinations are influenced, or altered, by the intellectual and emotional fuel that we constantly feed it.

It is extremely important to feed your mind with constructive thoughts because your subconscious mind will continuously work towards achieving what you have impressed upon it. The subconscious mind does not distinguish between right and wrong, good and bad, true or false, and will interpret and respond according to how we have consciously fed it over our lifetime. The American essayist Ralph Waldo Emerson said: "Man is what he thinks all day long."

The subconscious mind also contains our self-identity and how we see ourselves. This internal representation of ourselves is of paramount importance. The reason it is so important is because our subconscious has an internal mechanism that works in a similar fashion to a thermostat. This mechanism regulates our behaviour and actions in order to be consistent with our self-identity. The strongest desire within the human makeup is to remain consistent with our own identity. How we see ourselves is much more significant than what other people say or think about us.

Our self-identity and self-image is also responsible, to a large degree, for our personal health. It is important to have a healthy internal representation of ourselves because our internal mechanism will, over the long-term, regulate our behaviour accordingly. It will do this to remain consistent with our own internal self-identity.

I have believed for some time that certain labels can be both limiting, and damaging, when they pertain to people and their situations because they can affect our self-image. I didn't realize how potent they were until I watched a pantomime event at Independence '92. Independence '92 was an international event held in Vancouver and involved over three thousand people, with a variety of disabilities, from all over the world. Rick Hansen, who had previously become well known for his Man in Motion World Tour, chaired this event.

I didn't know what I was watching at the time, but I later realized that what I had watched in 1992 would stay with me for life. Let me set the scene for you. The pantomime was in process when I was on my way to a panel presentation on the history of the Canadian Charter of Rights and Freedoms. I decided to stop and enjoy the entertainment that was being provided by these hard-working performers. The skit was about a street person who was reaching out for a helping hand as people were busily going to and fro. Nobody stopped to assist this unfortunate individual. The pantomime was being done to the Phil Collins' song "Another Day in Paradise." The performance was masterfully done and looked very professional.

At the end of the performance each actor and actress took a bow to the audience and collectively were rewarded with a curtain call. After the curtain call, each performer gave his or her name and where they lived. There were nine performers in total and they were all from Hawaii. When they introduced themselves, they said their names in the following manner: "My name is Mary. I am a manic depressive and I live in Maui." The next person would say, "My name is Joe. I am a schizophrenic and I live in Honolulu." On it went until all nine performers had introduced themselves by name, label and place of residence.

Based on what I had witnessed when watching their talented performance, I didn't have a clue that these individuals were anything other than outstanding performers. As soon as they said, "I am" they seemed to physiologically change before my very eyes. This kept gnawing at me for a couple of years until I was able to understand more fully the power of labels and their association with our personal identity.

We can change our internal representation of ourselves by first consciously setting goals and objectives. We then must consistently and consciously affirm these goals and objectives until they are firmly implanted in our subconscious. When they are implanted and become a part of our metabolism our self-identity will be changed and our behaviour will follow to be consistent with this new identity. Therefore we must picture ourselves the way we want to be; otherwise we will by default have given up our health to the forces of life.

When we understand the importance of our beliefs and how they are reflected in our thoughts, we can see how they are impressed upon our subconscious mind, which acts accordingly. We can also begin to understand the role of our subconscious mind and its impact on our general health, and on our ability to heal our body, both physically and emotionally. With this understanding you and I now have additional knowledge which can positively contribute to our health and well-being.

Our subconscious mind is always working on our behalf and I can think of several practical situations that have been effectively handled by my subconscious. When I need a telephone number or the name of somebody who I have met some time ago, my subconscious mind invariably gives me the answer. I am sure we can all think of examples of when our subconscious mind has come up with creative solutions to a variety of needs or problems.

In my case I had often thought about how I would resolve the bathing problem if I ever decided to move out of the Aberhart Centre. It was easy for me to use the toilet and take a bath as long as I was in an accessible and appropriately designed facility such as the Aberhart. However, when I travelled or went visiting overnight, bathing and sometimes toileting became problematic for me. I would often consciously think of ways to practically resolve the bathing issue but could never seem to come up with an answer that would suit my needs. For a variety of reasons the conventional solutions such as wheel-in showers and expensive lifting devices were just not appropriate for me because of my scoliosis (curvature of the spine) and other physical frailties. I must have ruminated over this problem for several years, with no satisfactory solution coming to mind.

I am pleased to tell you that the moment I decided to get married and move out of the Aberhart is the day that my subconscious mind delivered to me the answer to my bathing requirements. The solution was both practical and inexpensive (Cdn $300). I have only my subconscious mind to thank for this useful bit of creativity that has changed and improved my quality of life immeasurably. We all have heard the biblical saying "Ask and ye shall receive." And that is precisely what our subconscious mind attempts to do on our behalf, particularly if we know how to program it and use it wisely.

VISUALIZATION

Visualization is an important tool in the bank of resources that each one of us has and is available to us when doing virtually any task. It can be significant in our individual ability to address illness and to assist in the curative process. I have listened to countless numbers of tapes and read several accounts of people utilizing the skill of visualization to facilitate the healing process. It has been used in both physical and emotional healing.

Einstein was quoted as saying: "Imagination is more important than knowledge."

We can see this in the innocence and curiosity of children who embody the significance of this quote in their every action. Imagination and visualization go together like a hand in a well fitting glove. Nowhere is this more powerful than when it is applied to the healing and curative process. Visualization is not always easy to apply effectively, but I am convinced that it is something that we can all learn to do. It all starts with our ability to imagine and see things the way that we want them to be. This is well articulated by Wayne Dyer in his book *You Will See It When You Believe It.*

Both imagination and visualization have proven to be crucial to the establishing of goals and in man's ability to accomplish them. The same principles that we use in goal setting are applicable when applied in the area of health. We first must imagine what we want and how we want it to be. This will establish our goal and then we can use the process of visualization to make the imagined outcome a reality. This may take a period of time, depending on what part of our body that we are focusing on. The reason for this is that different parts of our body regenerate at different rates.

There is a large body of research available on the subject of cellular replacement and regeneration which takes place within our bodies during every moment of our lifetime. It is this cellular regeneration which allows our body to repair itself, from the healing of a sore on our skin to the growing of a new liver. For example, our red blood cells are completely replaced within a 120-day period. It takes approximately six weeks to replace liver cells and within one year ninety-eight per cent of our body's cells are replaced with new cells.

This means that if we are diagnosed with a tumour this year, one year from now it will be a different tumour even though it may appear as if it is the same one as before. This is because the tumour is made up of cells and as the cells die from the old tumour they are replaced with new cells, thus the different tumour from one year to the next. This is a simplified explanation that is detailed much more eloquently by notable authors and experts in mind/body/soul medicine, authors such as Dr. Deepak Chopra (*Quantum Healing* and *Ageless Body, Timeless Mind*).

The opportunity to utilize visualization in the cellular regeneration process is available to each and every one of us and should not be under-rated nor discounted. It has been proven that our thoughts affect our biochemistry, which is all part of the body's regeneration process. Therefore, it can be reasoned that we have the inherent ability to affect and specify targeted benefits through the process of visualization. I believe this is an area of health and healing that can be further exploited and simplified in order to facilitate its ease of use in the self-curative process.

As for me, I am still experimenting with visualization, particularly when I get respiratory tract infections. My ability to impact a positive outcome in this area of personal treatment has been mixed. I have had good results from visualization when I am totally focused and concentrating effectively on the desired results. Throughout my life I have used visualization to picture myself running, throwing a ball, swinging a bat and even driving a vehicle. I have been accused of all kinds of back seat activity by those closest to me. Even my wife has accused me of such things on occasion. One day she said to me with a silly look on her face, "Are you back seat vacuuming?" I guess I was and now that has become a familiar phrase that she uses to remind me that I should keep my visualizations to myself!

I don't always learn my lessons easily. One day in downtown Vancouver, Valerie was trying to park our three-quarter-ton van in a tight parking space in a hotel parkade. She wasn't having much success and, because I had just finished driving, so to speak, about 1,400 kilometres from Edmonton to Vancouver from the back seat, I was confident that I could do a better job of parking than she was doing. Of course I made the big mistake of commenting to her that she should maybe try this approach or that approach.

I guess she wasn't in a very approachable state because she said in a very sarcastic tone "Okay, fine. You park the van then." She had called my bluff and if I didn't take her up on her offer I wouldn't be able to "back seat" anything again, and I was sure I couldn't keep my mouth shut that long!

I had no choice, I had to take up the challenge as presented.

I said, "Okay, I will if you will do the driving and follow my instructions." She looked somewhat surprised and said, "Okay, go ahead." I then proceeded to direct her, beginning with backing into the parking stall instead of going nose first. The long and short of this story is that I was able to efficiently and effectively guide the parking of our van through Valerie, who was my arms and legs in this ordeal. Not only that but I was able to accomplish this on the first attempt.

Valerie had acquired a newfound respect for my back seat driving ability. As far as I was concerned this was great because she finally cracked a smile, gave me a big kiss and, not only that, I had retained my ability to voice my suggestions from the back seat with confidence. I had also gained a newfound respect for my latent talent. I must admit that I am much more conscious of and discerning before putting my two cents worth in now. I guess we both came out ahead on the exchange.

The whole point of sharing this story is to illustrate the potency of visualization and its application to any given experience or happening in our lives. When it comes to our health, visualization combined with imagination can yield tremendous results on our behalf. First we must master the art, techniques and skill of visualization, and be able to teach and transfer these lessons through the teaching of others on a large scale so that everyone may benefit. One of the great things about visualization is that the skills are transferable to other areas and aspects of our lives.

In the future I believe that research into the potency of visualization will be supported by such tools as dark field microscopy through live blood cell analysis. Live blood cell analysis allows a technician to analyze a person's blood and display the tests on a television monitor, so that the individual who is being tested can see what is actually taking place in their blood. This visual demonstration has an important place in assisting an individual in understanding what actually takes place within his or her bodily system and what they can do to affect a positive health outcome. By way of example, a person can actually see the white blood cell activity as it fights off and attempts to destroy bacteria and infections.

My exposure to this technology showed me the possibilities of applying visualization to assist the white blood cell activity in fighting disease and warding off foreign invaders. If we understand how our white blood cells work, and have a picture of this activity in our mind, we should then be able to accelerate and enhance the activity of the cells through visualization.

In theory, when we know what organs in our body are under bacterial or viral attack, we should be able to affect white blood cell activity. By using visualization and mental imagery, combined with a picture of what a healthy organ should look like, we can begin to directly influence health and healing. Hopefully this will give you an idea of where visualization fits into the healing process and how we can combine it with a better understanding of our body as we begin to take control of our health through self responsibility.

SPIRITUAL NEEDS

"All hope cannot be pinned on science, technology and economic growth. The victory of technological civilization has also instilled a spiritual insecurity in us. Its gifts enrich, but enslave us as well...all is a struggle for material things, but an inner voice tells us that we have lost something pure, elevated and fragile. We have ceased to see the purpose. Let us admit, even if in a whisper and only to ourselves: in this bustle of life at breakneck speed—what are we living for?"

—Aleksandr Solzhenitsyn (Russian author)

I have not been a religious person up until this point in my life, but I have evolved into a person who has strong spiritual beliefs. When I was younger I had difficulty distinguishing between the two. When I was introduced to religion at a very young age it had very little meaning for me. If I went to church, listened to a reading of the Bible, or even when I got baptized, it was just something that I was supposed to do and could really have cared less whether I went through these rituals or not.

When I got polio, the ministry was prevalent on the polio ward in the form of a Catholic priest and a minister (in most cases from the United Church) representing the other religions in the form of hosting non-denominational services. I think these representatives of the church were assigned this responsibility in addition to other duties at their respective churches. Their presence was more related to bad news in the form of the administering of last rites or leading prayers for those who were dying.

In my teen years I became more involved in Bible study, primarily due to the influence of a roommate's mother, who was a very strong Lutheran. He and I were about the same age and often did things together. Also, the various churches would take an interest in the people on our ward by having members of their congregations either visit or do volunteer work. This was the beginning of a very confusing time for me as I tried to figure out life and its meaning. When I was younger, like all children I would ask questions and in most cases would be satisfied with simple nondescript or noncommittal answers. Now that I was a teenager the questions weren't necessarily any more sophisticated but the answers became more important to me.

I was confused for various reasons. I was trying to rationalize what I was experiencing, either directly, or through my many roommates, the trauma and challenges that were presented and why. Of course, I now realize that when you ask a "Why?" question, particularly as it relates to theology, there are few definitive answers. The meaning of life and who or what was God, became questions that wouldn't go away. The more questions I asked, the more confused I became. These thoughts were further complicated when I tried to interpret what made one religion better than another religion. Also, it seemed that some faiths treated certain individuals differently than others, and yet we were all supposed to be equals according to the scriptures. I was taught that baptism was necessary to enter the Kingdom of God (or Heaven) when we die. If this was the case, people who were very dear to me, including members of my family, were not going to go to heaven because they hadn't been baptized. And what about all those other people in other parts of the world? And what about babies who die? So many questions and so few answers.

Another reason I was confused was because I was beginning to wrestle with my own sexuality and all the stimulating hormonal challenges that this can present to a young and curious teenager. In addition, my situation was complicated due to my paralysis, respiratory condition, lack of privacy (as I was in a public ward), lack of support, lack of education and understanding. I began to be preoccupied with good-looking women and girls, but somehow I was thought of as less than a sexual being by those in authority, which translated into "Don't get your hopes up."

Looking at the opposite sex with lewd intent somehow seemed in contradiction with the moral lessons that I was learning through my biblical teachings and prejudices of others. This contradiction created an internal tug-of-war, to the point that I thought I might go to hell simply for thinking so-called evil thoughts, or for looking at a nice pair of legs. I was not only confused, I was beginning to get screwed up.

It was at this point in my life that I was close to depression and that could have led to more severe forms of mental illness. Fortunately for me, I decided to listen to my own feelings and thoughts, rather than to what was being almost force-fed me in the form of doctrine and the beliefs of others. I was able to acknowledge my feelings and take control, giving me a level of comfort that translated into me being a happy and reasonably well-adjusted individual.

I didn't abandon the importance of God in my life, even though I didn't know who or what, He/She/It was. Since that time, I have had an ongoing internal relationship with a part of me that I am still learning about. I am grateful that I have lived long enough to come to a level of spiritual understanding where purpose, meaning, the presence of God (however we personally define it) and most things that happen now make some semblance of sense to me.

What is right for me may not be right for others, but I have come to a place in my life where I am closer to being at peace with the innermost part of me than I have ever been before. The question of "Who am I, really?", is one that is continuing to reveal a part of me that I previously was not in touch with. This is a question, I believe, to which we all seek the answer at an individual level, even though we may not realize it. When we take the time to delve into this question, we will get in touch with our soul and our spirit, which I believe is who we really are.

The research on mind/body/soul strongly suggests that this innermost part of us is paramount in the healing process of our health, whether it is psychological, physical, emotional or spiritual. I believe this understanding is so important for the health of our families, our communities and ourselves.

In the 1997 January issue of *Perspectives*, the regular publication put out by the Alberta Association of Registered Occupational therapists, my friend Paul MacDonald, BScOT, wrote a feature article on occupational therapy and working with the soul. It is with his permission that I share this excerpt from what he had to say:

> The concept of the soul and spirit is slippery and difficult to capture in one definition. It attends to the invisible factors of life and exists outside the realm of the rational mind and concrete reality.

> Nonetheless, we can learn to sense its needs as we do with our biological endowments. The spirit is the energy of the soul enabling its presence to be felt. The soul is not a theory, but a quality or a dimension of experiencing life and ourselves. It has to do with depth, value, relatedness and personal substance. Words capture only a glimpse of the soul, but much of it remains and must remain a mystery.

> In addition, the soul is a source of immense power and is the seat and the source of life. Its power can be creative or destructive, gentle or aggressive. Harnessing the power of the soul requires one to integrate its reality and needs with those of our physical world. This integration involves living with grace and embracing all of life's experiences thereby harnessing the power and the mystery of the soul. Through embracing the experience of adversity and suffering artfully and with imagination, this integration is allowed to occur.

He concludes:

> There is value to be found in the lived experience of coping with illness and disability. This runs contrary to the medical model which views illness and disability as the enemy to be vanquished.

Unfortunately, our fast-paced North American lifestyle does not lend itself well to this need and understanding. In order to get to know and understand ourselves at the deepest level, we need to spend time with ourselves. For most of us this can be an uncomfortable or scary experience in that it takes an introspective in-depth dialogue between ourselves and our Creator. When we take the time to do this there will be healthy outcomes.

I mentioned earlier that I was not particularly religious, but I do have a healthy respect for the basics that are taught by most religions. I interpret them as being love for our fellow man, forgiveness, caring, sharing, generosity and giving of ourselves to others unselfishly and without ulterior motives. Obviously, these are very high ideals and ones that few of us mortal beings live up to. Just think about it. If we did this on a daily basis at an individual level, what a difference it would make in our personal relationships, work environment, community and in the world. No doubt the health of each and every one of us would be significantly impacted.

Until I began to study the power and potential of mind/body/soul implications for health, I guess I didn't really value and appreciate many of the biblical teachings that I had heard when I attended various church services. I sort of considered the teachings that love conquers all and forgiveness of others on more of a surface level, rather than at my deepest personal roots. I now realize and firmly believe that love and forgiveness are the answers to virtually every ill that we have, whether on a personal or societal level.

The further we get away from these fundamental basics, the more out of balance our lives–individually and collectively–become. The teaching, "We reap what we sow" keeps coming back to me. I believe that if I want things to change in my life, then first I must change. In my view, this applies to all of us. Until we as a society get back to these fundamentals, we will continue to have increasing health challenges, both as individuals and at the socioeconomic and political levels.

I have come to the conclusion that the only antidote to hate is love; that the release from most of our own personal prisons will come through forgiveness of others and of ourselves. If we gave ourselves these two gifts on a regular basis, most of us would release a ton of psychological and emotional baggage. This in turn would pave the way for healing, prevention and improved health.

In Ghandi's autobiography, *My Experiments With Truth*, he talks about a Gujarati didactic stanza, its precept being–return good for evil. This became his guiding principle. It became such a passion with him that he began numerous experiments in it. Here are those wonderful lines that he lived by:

For a bowl of water give a goodly meal;
For a kindly greeting bow thou down with zeal;
For a simple penny pay thou back with gold;

If thy life be rescued, life do not withhold;
Thus the words and actions of the wise regard;
Every little service tenfold they reward,
But the truly noble know all men as one,
And return with gladness good for evil done.

I know this is extremely difficult, but if we look around us we can see the negative consequences of hanging on to negative influences and emotions, through vindictiveness, grudges, revenge or anything similar. This appears to be a natural human response when someone hurts us, either physically or emotionally. We are all guilty of saying or doing things in the heat of the moment that we later regret. Some of us never let go of these feelings, and they no doubt will manifest themselves in compromised health, in ways that we cannot even fathom.

In my experience of living and working with people who have disabilities or medical conditions that have sometimes been precipitated through no obvious fault of their own, I have seen the extremes of which I speak. Those people who continue to blame the system or to blame others, whether they be people in their immediate circle of influence or not, get stuck and literally are unable to move forward in their lives in a constructive manner. Conversely, those who have "let go" have fared much better in many ways, including their overall health, both socially and economically. For me there is a strong message in this example and one which we can all learn from. I don't intend to sound pious nor do I mean to preach, but I do want people to know and realize that daily, what we think, do and feel towards ourselves and others has significant health implications.

Our spirituality is a journey that began before we were born and will continue after we physically depart from this world. Talking about physical, I believe the physical part of us is over-rated in its importance, and I speak with some authority as a person who continues to live with the challenges and benefits of quadriplegia. You may well ask, "What benefits?" My response is that whenever life appears to throw me a curve ball, and if I face it squarely and can come through it, there may be some scars, but I will be forced to deal with elements of my being that I may have otherwise ignored. In many ways, this has made me a much stronger person.

At this point I would like to share with you an excerpt from my address to the graduating students at our convocation. This is when I received my Honorary Doctor of Laws degree from the University of Alberta Senate.

I want you in the audience to know, even though I have been awarded an honorary doctorate from such a prestigious university, it hasn't necessarily meant a corresponding respect from my immediate family or my close friends. For example, my son was conversing in the backyard with a friend of mine and my friend said to my son, "Did you know that your daddy is an important man?" Jamie, my son, paused and then casually said, "I'm four and a half!" To get ready for this occasion it was necessary to get measured for the cap and gown. I asked my wife to measure the circumference of my head. She took the tape measure and wrapped it around my head and I asked her what size it was. She said, in her smart-aleck way, "Getting bigger."

When I was asked to give the convocation address it was suggested that you might like to hear a bit about my life. So in the next few minutes I will attempt to share some of the things that have been most meaningful to me.

I was preoccupied with being unhealthy in the sense that I couldn't see all the possibilities for myself that I would discover later in life. My life changed when I changed. It changed when I decided to take control of my life and my actions. I was not a particularly compliant patient and, consequently, I had to learn a great deal about diplomacy, politics and working with people in order to get things done. Being dependent on others for some of my daily needs proved to be a great teacher.

Specifically, I began to have respect for others and recognize that I could learn from everyone I met no matter who they were. Basically, it was up to me to take care of my health and not my doctor's responsibility. It was up to me to be active and to learn the things that I needed to learn in order to be a fully participating member of society. I also learned that by modelling others who were successful and learning from other's hard earned lessons, commonly called mistakes, that I could make progress much more quickly and not waste my time or my energy.

With this attitude I began to build a personal library of references which, in turn, boosted my confidence. Another important piece of learning was when I began to effectively manage my negative emotions. I recognized that four of the most useless emotions that a person could have were the feelings of guilt, jealousy, envy and worry. I worked hard to handle these feelings and I believe that in doing so it has made me much more appreciative of everyone that I come into contact with.

An emotion that we all experience is fear. Often it is fear of the unknown. I read somewhere, do that which you are afraid of and you will be afraid no longer. I don't always practice this but just being aware has made me meet many challenges head on rather than trying to ignore them.

The greatest gift that a university degree has given you is the ability to learn. I want to suggest to you that this is only the beginning. Because of the microchip, knowledge and information has been estimated to be doubling every eighteen months, rendering some industries obsolete. For instance, who would have ever believed that the vinyl record industry would disappear virtually overnight? Think about it. This could mean that what you have learned in university will only be a fraction of what you need to learn in order to function effectively in the twenty-first century. It is absolutely imperative that we all commit ourselves to a process of continuous learning, which means that we must keep an open mind on virtually all subjects. The reason we must do this is because the perceived truth changes. What was true yesterday is not necessarily true today and may not be true tomorrow. We are in a state of continuous change including our beliefs, our attitudes, our physical bodies and even our friends.

One of the greatest teachers in life is adversity. Anyone that has gone through or faced adversity has usually come out a stronger person. Bill Marriot said: "Good timber doesn't grow with ease, the stronger the wind, the stronger the trees."

Yet adversity is something that we all fear, and something we try to avoid at all costs. Adversity is inevitable and something we will all face in our lives. My experience has taught me that if it is not possible to embrace adversity, then we must at least align with it. It was Napolean Hill who said: "With every adversity comes a seed of an equivalent or greater benefit."

Our task then, is to take the adversity and turn it into a positive situation by taking the lessons that it teaches us and applying it in our lives for the benefit of ourselves and others.

In my case, I learned that the physical part of life can be over-rated. Adversity can put you in touch with the deepest part of your being–your soul and your spirit. This is really who we are. Wayne Dyer puts it another way when he says: "We are not a physical being having a spiritual experience, but rather a spiritual being having a human experience."

In closing, I quote from an unknown source who says: "Yesterday is history, tomorrow is a mystery, and today is a gift. That is why it is called 'the present'. Use it wisely!"

All my life I thought that if I just had a certain amount of money then I would be set. When I attained that certain amount of money I then had another dollar figure in mind, and each time I reached the next dollar figure, I realized that I needed and wanted more. It wasn't until I met a man who had built a multi-million-dollar business that I recognized the folly of this thinking. This gentleman, I'll call him Jack, had built his business to the point that he commanded and got, two hundred million dollars for his financial edifice, which was operating in North America at the time of sale.

Jack sold his business when his health started to deteriorate. His health deterioration was presented primarily through the manifestation of rheumatism and cancer. I met Jack at an international event, and before the event was very far along he had told everybody about his situation, his money and his life.

Jack's emotional needs were sadly obvious as he tried to buy love and friendship, which he craved, desired, and as we all do, needed. I also observed that he was really hurting at a deep emotional level, because on more than one occasion he brought up the same subject. I knew from my work that it was a personal and family issue that would be very difficult for anyone to handle.

In my view, his emotional needs were being expressed publicly because he hadn't dealt with this particular issue that had started some thirty-seven years previously, and which continued to trouble him. Even though it was not apparent to him, it seemed obvious to me, and at the time I shared in his grief.

He had failed to grasp the simple fact that a person can't buy the important things in life; they can only acquire them through trust, honesty, sincerity, letting go and, most of all, through love itself.

It was at this time that I realized that I was wealthier than Jack would ever be, even though he was financially richer than I could ever imagine myself being. The reason is, health is wealth. If we could only grasp the fact that individual wealth, in a meaningful sense, is expressed emotionally, psychologically, physically and spiritually. It is then that we can consider ourselves truly healthy.

MEDITATION

What are some of the things that we can do to combat stress? This question becomes even more relevant in this fast-paced world, a world in which people have something in common with a hamster. The commonality is that we often find ourselves on a treadmill, and we just keep going at a faster and faster pace.

In self-defence and to unleash the hamster within, an increasing number of people are turning to meditation and they are experiencing positive results. Meditation has long been practised by other cultures, but North Americans are just now beginning to experience what many have known for centuries. Not only is meditation a relief and escape from everyday stress, but it means that the individual who practices these meditation techniques also gets to spend time with themselves. Often this can be very therapeutic.

Transcendental Meditation (TM) is known to Westerners as primarily, a relaxation exercise. TM is an abbreviated version of a meditation used in certain Hindu sects to detach from the here and now and establish a connection with a greater consciousness that exists outside of space and time. It is this greater consciousness that animates the universe.

We Western types have often attempted to escape the stress-filled world by attempting to reconnect with nature. We may do this through camping, hiking or fishing. The reason we try to reconnect with nature is because it is very refreshing. Contact with nature can be helpful in recharging our natural energies.

In a way it seems ironic that we would work our tails off so that we can pursue materialism and, at the same time, attempt to save enough money to go on holidays, or spend weekends near nature. Whether it be in the mountains, beside a lake or along some hiking trail admiring and smelling Mother Nature's magnificent aromas. What is ironic is that our political, business, environmental and policy decisions are making it increasingly difficult to connect with nature. These decisions have not always been in the best interest of people, or animals, even though they may have made good economic sense at the time of decision. As a consequence of these decisions, our options for escape from stress are becoming increasingly more difficult to pursue, even as we need this escape and reconnection with nature now more than ever.

We can take a lesson from the North American Indian who respects the land and its offerings because it is truly the provider of everything we need and have. They know the value of, and cherish the connection with, nature and the creator of our universe, which is very important in health and the elimination of stress.

THE POWER OF PRAYER

Prayer can be another form of meditation and like meditation has proven to be extremely useful in the healing process. In her feature article on faith and healing in the 24 June 1996 issue of *Time* magazine, Claudia Wallis looked at the question: Can prayer, faith, and spirituality really improve your physical health? She found that a growing and surprising body of scientific evidence says they can. Although skeptics abound, a growing number of researchers, physicians and scholars are discovering what spiritual leaders have said all along–prayer can be potent medicine.

The body and mind used to be separate realms because doctors spent the last century trying to rid Western medicine of remnants of mysticism, something Sigmund Freud dismissed as "infantile helplessness." Today many physicians encourage their patients to communicate with their God or their Creator. Some doctors even pray with their patients.

"Nearly three hundred studies dating back to the 1890s touch directly or indirectly on the role of religion in healing," says Dr. David Larson, a research psychiatrist formerly at the National Institute of Health. He further estimates that about eighty per cent of the studies show that deeply held religious beliefs positively affect health.

In her article, Ms. Wallis asks the question: Could it be that religious faith has some direct influence on physiology and health?

She cautions, of course, that although the American Medical Association has nothing against prayer, the organization opposes spiritual therapy that delays or replaces traditional medical treatment.

Masaharu Taniguchi PhD, in his book *The Magic of Truth–Truth of Life, Volume 1*, confirms that love, words of love and praise are responsible for giving life its nourishment. However, he believes its true power does not truly apply until it is expressed through prayer. Prayer seems to be particularly effective when it is complemented with words of love and praise. It must be remembered that words are all-powerful and that they can be expressed through prayer, both silently and out loud. Many very interesting books have been written about the power of prayer. For your information, a doctor who has become well recognized for his writings, and who has devoted his career to studying research into the power of prayer, is internist Larry Dossey, the author of the 1993 best-seller *Healing Words*.

On Christmas Eve 1996, the *Calgary Herald* newspaper carried a series of articles on spirituality and prayer written by columnist Gordon Legge. He wrote that Larry Dossey, in his 1996 release *Prayer Is Good Medicine* (HarperCollins), found that there were some 130 studies that have looked at the link between prayer and healing. He also mentioned that it doesn't matter who prays, or what denomination or religion is involved. It can all have a positive effect on other people's health. This is particularly true when unconditional love and caring are involved. These books are an excellent read and should convince even the greatest skeptic that there are hidden powers in prayer.

Prayer, like almost everything in life, can also provide us with moments of humour. My mother shared a story about getting out of her car and loading up her arms with materials for a meeting just before locking her car door. She had no sooner locked the car door when she noticed the car beginning to roll forward. At this point she realized that she had forgotten to put on the emergency brake or ensure that the car's standard drive was in gear. With few options available to her, she tried to re-enter the car by attempting to insert the key into the lock while trying to move at the same pace as the car. All this while she was carrying an armful of meeting materials.

By this time, however, the car was rolling a little faster, making it more difficult for mom to insert the key. There seemed little that she could do other than to watch the impending collision, as her red Ford Tempo headed towards a more expensive white vehicle that was parked in the direction her car was headed. Suddenly, as she silently prayed, and to her amazement, her car stopped rolling about two inches short of hitting the nice white car. See, prayer does have its benefits as well as moments of humour!

Our
Natural
Balance

I believe that most things in life have a natural balance, and this includes our total being. I further believe that at the moment conception takes place we are in total alignment with all aspects of our being, including our spiritual connection. In my view, every time we do or say something that is incongruent with this spiritual connection, or in other words who we really are, we incrementally move further out of alignment and away from our natural alignments. I say alignments because we have a natural body balance, which includes psychological, emotional, physical and spiritual requirements.

To illustrate my point, I share with you a story about a gentleman who was recovering from multiple sclerosis. He called it, "voluntary simplicity," and said it was part of his recovery. He believes the simplest way to recover from MS, or any immune condition, is to adopt a natural lifestyle and diet. The reason is because our systems are out of balance because we live under pressure to consume and produce and have no real connection to serving our fellow humans. In other words, he thinks we are spiritually and physically bankrupt.

This gentleman's approach is spiritual in nature, based on his belief that each individual is linked to all others, that we are all cells in the body of God, or universe, whichever you prefer. The key for this gentleman is that it is important to understand that each person/cell derives all its nutrients from the whole and performs a useful function for the whole.

You have probably heard or read that all human beings are born equal. You may agree or disagree with this perspective. I happen to agree with it to a point. I think that we are born equal in that we are all spiritual beings and that we are all inherently good at birth. The moment we are influenced by our earthly presence and surrounding environment is the moment that equality changes and that inequality begins to occur. In addition, we are not necessarily born into equitable surroundings or situations and this further complicates, or can even compromise, our chances to remain in a healthy balance.

A natural balance also applies to society and its components. It is when society or elements of society become out of balance or out of alignment, that individual difficulties begin to manifest themselves as society's problems. I use the analogy of a wheel alignment on a vehicle to illustrate my point. Most people are familiar with the need to take care of our motor vehicles in order that they don't wear out prematurely, and as part of the care we often have the wheels aligned and balanced. We do this for obvious reasons; reasons such as to prevent the tires from wearing unevenly and, more importantly, to prevent unnecessary deterioration of the entire vehicle by ensuring that it operates smoothly and efficiently. Without the wheels being aligned and balanced, the entire health of the vehicle would be prematurely and unnecessarily compromised.

Traditional Chinese medicine (TCM) and Ayurvedic medicine work with the individual's natural body balance with the view to re-establishing the natural balance of that person's body. TCM takes into consideration that our physical body has a parallel energy structure. TCM works with this natural energy system in a variety of ways, the most common being the use of acupuncture and Qi Gong (*chee gong*).

Ayurvedic medicine works on the premise that our body has a natural balance that is made up of what is referred to as doshas. The three doshas are Vata, Pitta and Kapha. Each person has a natural occurring blend of these doshas and this blend is specific to each individual. Depending on each person, one of these doshas will be more dominant than the other two, but all will be present and are interrelated and interdependent with the others. In these two approaches to medicine the presence of optimal health is directly related to the energy systems and doshas being in balance. These approaches to medicine practice are considerably different than allopathic or Western medicine, which primarily works separately with the physical, emotional and mental aspects of our being.

When we are out of physical alignment the signs are often fairly obvious. Signs such as a bad back, joint pain or sore muscles are very common. The signs that are not so obvious are things that for the most part we cannot see, and yet they may have more significant and devastating consequences if left unattended. These other signs may eventually manifest themselves in physical ailments later in life. They may include unresolved issues around relationships, abuse, trust, honesty and many others that are too numerous to mention here. The point is, every time we tell a lie, cheat or some other action that is inconsistent or incongruent with our spiritual or true self, we become further misaligned with ourselves. This is the beginning of illness and disease, but also these actions can unknowingly prevent us from being happy. Until they are consciously addressed or resolved, these actions can often hold us back from progressing with our lives.

I often think of this misalignment as a maze in which we have become lost and must try to return to our true beginnings. These true beginnings could take on an individual interpretation but, in essence, are who we really are. In other words, these true beginnings make up our soul. Every time we do something to further the misalignment process, the maze becomes more complex and it becomes more difficult to navigate our way back to our true beginnings. Once we become so far out of personal alignment, or out of balance, we may experience symptoms of illness and disease that have been manifesting for a considerable length of time. It may depend on which area of our life is out of alignment, i.e. spiritual, psychological or physical, but rest assured the symptoms expressed by the human body and its various mechanisms are very seldom the cause. The symptoms that become visible to us through the process of disease, is our opportunity to look for and address the root cause of this manifestation.

In this section I am going to share some personal thoughts, observations and experiences that I have learned from others, and various bits of information that I have gleaned from reading.

OUR IMMUNE SYSTEM

"The doctor of the future will give no medicine, but will interest his patients in the care of the human frame, in diet and in the cause and prevention of disease."

—Thomas Alva Edison

The human body is an amazing machine and one that we are unlikely to ever fully understand. We do know, however, that a healthy immune system is the key to maintaining our health and vitality. It is when our immune system becomes weakened that we become susceptible to all kinds of unwanted bacterial and biological disturbances. I'd had polio many years before I understood what the immune system actually was or what it did. Because I didn't understand the role and importance of a healthy immune system, I didn't know how to optimize it or work in harmony with it. My sense is that this lack of basic understanding regarding the immune system affects most of us. We learn minimal amounts about health when we go to primary school and, in most cases, this information is outdated or of little consequence for the larger picture of our personal health.

A healthy immune system is our defence against unwanted illness and disease. If we find ourselves battling an unwanted condition it is because our immune system is in need of repair. So it behoves us to work with it and keep it as strong as we possibly can. There is no one solution or magic bullet to ensure a healthy immune system. However, by nurturing and working with our body and the psychological, physical, emotional and spiritual aspects of our being, we can often regulate and control our health results.

In the past we have looked to the pharmacist and drugs for quick answers to complex and often multiple problems that have been manifesting over time. If we look closely we can usually pinpoint changes that we can make in our lifestyle choices to give our immune system a chance to recover and restore its ability to defend us against unwanted intruders. Drugs and drastic treatments such as chemotherapy usually knock out our immune defences and are often the only weapons that allopathic medicine has to offer. We can work with our natural immune system through lifestyle choices, by eating properly through healthy food choices, and with whole food supplements that are now available. This will improve our chances for a healthier and happier life.

Another important reason for us to seriously consider supplementing our diet with quality products that have been maintained in their natural state is because of the by-products of technology. By this I mean such things as radio waves, radiation from computer screens, emissions from transmission lines, microwaves, infrared waves, pollution of our air and water, cellular telephones, car emissions and a whole host of other by-products of man-made technologies. We have continually improved our material products and the delivery systems that make them readily available for our everyday use. In this process we have not necessarily done a good job of understanding the need, nor have we always taken the necessary precautions, to limit or eliminate long-term damage to our environment and, as a consequence, to ourselves. In fairness to the advancement of technology, it is not always possible to gauge or predict negative consequences from things that make our materialistic lives better and more enjoyable.

We do know that every action has a reaction and results in a consequence that is known or unknown. We also know that virtually everything we do in life creates free radicals, which means that our bodies will have to deal with them whether they are a result of technology or natural bodily processes. Man's knowledge and ability to apply this knowledge is growing at an almost unbelievable rate. This knowledge allows us to create and harness technology like never before but, in harnessing technology, we also create unknowns that will impact on and dramatically change not only our lives, but our children's lives and those of many generations to come.

Over the centuries man has evolved, adjusted and adapted, as have other creatures in the world. Up until now, as a human species, we have been able to keep up and adapt to the negative environmental impacts that have been by-products of technological advancement. A number of large questions arise from the rapid advancement of technology that is happening today, especially when it is combined with globalization and the sharing of information. These factors mean that free radicals are being created at an increasing rate and are formulated from sources that are radically different from anything mankind has had to adjust and adapt to before.

The last forty years, and particularly the last ten, have presented challenges that our immune systems were probably not designed to handle. The simple lifestyle of our ancestors produced little stress, compared to that which most people are under today. This stress results from environmental, political, financial and sociological factors, and for most people are inescapable. This means that our immune systems are constantly being challenged, with very little chance for relief. Because much of what takes place is beyond individual control, and can only be influenced with collective actions, it becomes even more important that we use whatever tools and defences that are available to each one of us. It becomes more and more clear that we must bolster and maintain a strong immune system in order to prevent or limit unwanted illness. In my view, new health technologies in the form of supplements that are maintained in a natural state will be part of the answer.

STRESS

The late Dr. Hans Selye, the acknowledged father of stress research because of his work begun in the 1930s, once defined stress as "the non-specific response of the body to any demand made upon it." Dr. Deepak Chopra says that stress is our response to a physical or psychological fear.

We all have stress in our lives and sometimes it is useful stress because it creates the urgency that is needed to motivate us to do things. At other times stress can be detrimental to our health. In this case if we can understand the source of the stress, then we may be in a position to change, minimize or even eliminate it. The problem is not only identifying the stress source. Once the source has been identified, it is necessary to take personal action, and this may prove to be more difficult for us than its identification.

I think it is important that we understand that we have the capability and personal resources to handle virtually any stress or stressful situation in our lives. If we recognize and understand that we can affect the stress in our daily activities, then we can handle it with confidence. This is extremely important. According to some research that has been done on stress, it is estimated that somewhere between seventy-five and ninety per cent of all visits to doctors are for stress-related disorders. The same article said that forty per cent of employee turnover is due to stress and that eighty per cent of disease is now believed to be stress related. In addition, a twenty-year study conducted by the University of London School of Medicine has determined that unmanaged mental and emotional reactions to stress present a more serious health risk than cigarette smoking or eating high cholesterol foods (Source: *Access*, Mainstream Access Corp., Spring 1995, Vol. 4, Number 1).

ALLERGIES

Most of us experience, or have experienced, one or more allergies in our lifetime. The causes can be many and are very difficult if not impossible to identify. They range from severe and life threatening to mild and being a nuisance. Even though allergies are difficult to alleviate, once they have been identified they can often be controlled, or maybe even eliminated through a variety of remedies.

Two culprits that are all too common, and that can often be an underlying cause of several allergies, are *candida albicans* in the form of systemic candidiasis (commonly referred to as a yeast infection) and/or parasites. These causes are often overlooked when we are experiencing health problems—problems such as food allergies. Allergies often express themselves through a variety of conditions such as asthma, eczema, insomnia, palpitations, shortness of breath and anxiety attacks. These expressions can lead to severe medical challenges if left untreated. When we do treat them we often treat the symptoms rather than the cause, which helps relieve the discomfort, but does very little to correct the problem.

Yeast is naturally contained in our bodies and in our environment. The problem isn't that we have yeast, but that we have a yeast imbalance, which then begins to create health challenges. Parasites, like yeast, can also create a metabolic imbalance in our bodies, and are far more prevalent in our modern-day culture than we realize. There are many new and useful natural products on the market that effectively address these unwanted invaders of our body. I encourage you to do your own research regarding yeast and parasites. This will raise your comfort level and increase your knowledge. This information may be of value to you or to someone you know.

FREE RADICALS

Free radicals are something that most of us know very little about, yet they greatly affect each and every one of us. In fact, they are known to researchers as the culprits that are responsible for creating illness, disease, the aging process and other destructive activities within our bodies. "Free radical" is a descriptive label that will become a part of everyone's personal vocabulary.

Free radicals are formed through the body's natural metabolic processes and through the exchange of oxygen that occurs with breathing. Free radicals are created through a process of oxidization similar to the rusting of pipes, except this oxidization takes place within our bodies. These free radicals can damage our cells and tissues. While we cannot readily see what is happening in the body, everyday examples of oxidative free radical damage can be seen through the rusting of metal and the rapid browning of a cut apple. We can't avoid the creation of free radicals, but there are things we can do to minimize the damage caused by these undesirable by-products. This raises the obvious question–what can we do?

ANTIOXIDANTS

What are antioxidants, and how do they affect our health? Antioxidants are the agents that we need to combat free radicals and the damage that they can cause to our body. In recent years scientists have begun to establish links between oxidative free radical damage to the body's cells and tissues and the development of a number of chronic diseases such as arthritis, atherosclerosis, cancer, cataracts, heart disease and lung ailments. Antioxidants are essential to strengthening and maintaining a strong immune system. Antioxidants come in the form of vitamin C, betacarotene, vitamin E, vitamin A and selenium. They are also found in the natural properties contained in raw fruits and vegetables. It is this army of antioxidant elements that is our main weapon in strengthening our natural immune system against illness, disease and premature aging.

These antioxidants are only available to us through eating raw fruits and vegetables or by taking supplements that are available through a variety of vendors and direct marketing sources. Because it is difficult for us to eat the required quantity and variety of fresh fruits and vegetables on a daily basis, we will all need to seriously consider supplementing our daily food intake with supplements containing antioxidants. The closer to nature these supplements are, the more effective they will be for us.

SOIL DEPLETION AND MINERALS

Our approach to modern-day farming has resulted in large-scale operations that are mostly concerned with turning out large volumes of produce at the best price. It also requires the ability of farmers to compete globally and to adjust and adhere to the economic and profit pressures. These pressures have often put expediency ahead of good practices, practices such as replenishing and replacing minerals in the soil after crop cultivation. Our not-so-fertile farmland also falls prey to nature's elements in the form of wind and turbulence. With reference to current farming practices, I am reminded of the clear-cut logging practices that have raised the ire of environmental groups and resulted in high-profile public demonstrations. In my view, through many of our current farming approaches we are continuing the rape and pillage of our lands in the name of economics.

At this point I am reminded of a piece of prose by William Shakespeare, titled *Pardon Me:*

Thou bleeding piece of earth that I am meek and gentle with these butchers.

Dr. Joel Wallach, an author and speaker, has made it his life's work to share the importance of minerals to our health and longevity. In his writing and speeches he details specific connections of mineral deficiencies and a variety of medical conditions. He emphasizes that the importance of minerals in the diet is far too often overlooked. Minerals are necessary for ninety-five per cent of your/our body's daily functions. The body can function, however poorly, without vitamins, but without minerals the body will die. Your body naturally produces vitamins from its inherent mineral supply, so when minerals are also depleted, the body suffers. Because of soil depletion, poor crop rotation, loss of valuable topsoil due to flooding, and over-irrigation, much of the natural trace mineral content has been lost from today's food supply. In fact many of the fruits and vegetables that we daily consume contain fewer nutrients than in years gone by. This is because they are grown in soil that is deficient in essential minerals.

Some of the benefits a mineral-rich diet may include are increased energy levels, better assimilation and utilization of the foods we eat and the supplements we consume. When a body is lacking minerals, vitamins have little or no effect and, as a result, a health conscious individual needs to be aware of the importance of a diet that includes sufficient trace minerals, possibly through supplementation.

Professor Stephen Shoenthaler is with the California Department of Sociology and Criminal Justice. In 1996 he carried out an extensive research project involving convicts in the United States. His research found that, in his estimation, violence in prisons could be cut in half if prisoners were given a balanced diet. He said inmates in the studies had shortages of fourteen or fifteen nutrients, including many vitamins and some minerals. He concluded in his study that we can lower aggression either by giving prisoners a proper balanced diet or by leaving the diet alone and just by giving them a low dose of a very good multiple mineral supplement.

It is known that the body can function without vitamins but without minerals we can't survive. Some experts believe that mineral-starved foods threaten millions of Americans, despite the country's reputation of being the best-fed nation on earth.

During aging or illness, when the mineral supply is depleted, cell growth slows down and reproduction finally stops, resulting in death. The person is said to have died of natural causes and/or old age, whereas the cause may have been mineral deficiency. There are many amazing cases of regeneration from just the addition of minerals to the diet of an affected individual.

The late Dr. Linus Pauling, who was world renowned for his work with vitamin C and after whom the Linus Pauling Institute in the United States is named, claimed: "You can trace every sickness, every disease, and every ailment to a mineral deficiency."

LEADING CAUSES OF DEATH

The importance of vitamins, enzymes and minerals cannot be overstated. Obviously, it is becoming increasingly difficult to get what we need from dietary sources, and particularly from the average North American diet. This makes the case for supplements extremely powerful.

The following is a list of the ten most common causes of death in the US. Please note that this list does not include the 1998 University of Toronto study that says prescription drugs and iatrogenic (medically induced) illnesses are the fourth leading cause of death in the US.

1. Heart disease	39.5%
2. Cancer	28.7%
3. Stroke	8.5%
4. Chronic obstructive pulmonary	5.6%
5. Accidents and adverse effects	4.7%
6. Pneumonia and influenza	4.4%
7. Diabetes	3.1%
8. AIDS-related	2.2%
9. Suicide	1.6%
10. Liver disease	1.3%

Source: Monthly Vital Statistics Report, Vol. 45, no.3 (S2), Births and Deaths; United States, 1995.

As you can see from these statistics, roughly forty-eight per cent of the deaths in North America each year occur from heart disease and strokes. Just under thirty per cent occur as a result of cancer. The good news is that virtually all of the illnesses and diseases listed above can be impacted in a significant and positive way by the ways in which we nourish, nurture, treat and love ourselves. So what are you waiting for?

FOOD SUPPLEMENTS

These words come from award winning nutritionist, Ranjit Kumar Chandra of Memorial University of Newfoundland, in an editorial in the *Journal of the American Medical Association* (7 May 1997): "The era of nutritional supplements to promote health and reduce illness is here to stay."

My personal research has led me to realize the importance of supporting our diet with food supplements. The reasons seem to be increasing daily, and the evidence is mounting in support of supplementation. It is almost impossible for the average person, me included, to get the required nutrients and enzyme activity from eating a regular diet, even if the diet appears to be balanced. The reasons include erosion of the soil and the subsequent depletion of many necessary minerals, processing of foods, utilization of chemicals in farming and in food preservation, and the ripening of fruits and vegetables on grocery shelves. These are some of the reasons that our food is of poorer quality and lacking in many of the nutrients, both in quality and quantity that our bodies require.

There are many supplements that are now being marketed through commercial outlets, pharmacies, health food stores and a plethora of network marketing companies. Many of the products that are available provide benefits, ranging all the way from minimal to significant, for the individual taking them. However, like the many choices that we have when purchasing an automobile, or even a smaller ticket item, we need to shop around. Unfortunately this is easier said than done. When we want to purchase an automobile, we can ask questions, go for a test drive, talk to our family and friends regarding their experiences, look for a vehicle on a car lot or through a private sale, and generally take our time gathering information. This can all be done before we arrive at a level of comfort and sign on the dotted line.

It is not quite so simple when looking for information on products that will assist us with improving our health through preventative methods. In some ways a person might expect it to be easier because health is something that we should all be interested in. This is not always the case because of the lack of cohesive information and understanding which exists in this emerging and important area of health promotion and disease prevention. The vested interests that permeate both the medical and commercial aspects of health promotion present a confusing picture to even the most knowledgeable of individuals. Information is also becoming available at an increasing rate, which makes it doubly difficult to stay abreast of current knowledge. I believe that it is for these reasons that we owe it to ourselves to read, talk to other people, experiment, test products and generally to become as informed as we possibly can. The reasons we should do this are purely selfish in that our aim should be to take responsibility for our health, both for ourselves and our families.

Due to the influence of the medical culture on our personal health, we have overused and become dependent on prescription drugs and antibiotics when our immune system is under attack. This is about to change with the explosion of interest in the field of nutriceuticals and supplementation. The potential for targeted and/or combined dosages of antioxidants, enzyme therapy and phytochemicals is significant. There is now a growing number of players who are interested in developing products which will provide necessary, but unwanted, competition for the pharmaceutical industry.

The resulting usage of nutriceuticals for medicinal purposes could be similar to the ways in which antibiotics were historically used. The overall effectiveness of this approach has yet to be determined, but it promises to be better for our health, as nutriceuticals support and enhance the body's natural immune system in fighting off illness and disease. Antibiotics tend to destroy the naturally occurring flora (good bacteria) contained in the bowel, which is necessary for the immune system to function effectively.

The likelihood of a person taking too much of a nutriceutical product and overdosing is slim, when compared to pharmaceutical products. The reason is that very few nutriceuticals are toxic, even in a mega-dose. Nevertheless, there is always the danger that certain substances when ingested into the body may be problematic for some individuals and, if they are taken excessively or inappropriately, a person may become toxic.

Currently, we depend on doctors to determine what we need and to prescribe a regimen of pills and treatments, accordingly. The future will probably be different in that we, the general public, will need to take more personal responsibility for our own health and occasional treatment. The medical care system which we currently access for all sorts of aches, pains, illness, injury, disease and colds will still be available to us, but the usage of the medical system will be more specific to acute intervention and the need for emergency response.

Once the acute crisis is over it will be up to each one of us to work closely with our physician or trusted advisors, to find and facilitate a program that will be closely linked to diet, exercise and overall lifestyle. The solutions will depend heavily on nutriceuticals as part of the ongoing therapy and rehabilitation. The nutriceuticals will be of two main types in that they will be both general and specific in their purpose. The general nutriceuticals will be as close to nature as technology will allow and will contain a variety of natural vitamins, minerals, enzymes, antioxidants, phytochemicals and whatever else scientists discover and technology can encapsulate. The specific type of nutriceuticals will have an increased and targeted dosage of nutritional ingredients, which generally will have a beneficial effect, but more importantly, they will zero in on the areas of the body that are under attack from bacteria, viruses and disease. This is very similar to antibiotic treatment, but different in that they will work in harmony with the natural defences of the body rather than interfering with them.

It is almost impossible for even the most disciplined of eaters to get the required daily intake of nutrients, let alone for the rest of us. The most logical remedy is to take dietary supplements with our meals. This will assist us in digesting, absorbing and complementing the required nutrients from our food sources. The questions are what should we take, how many should we take, what quantities should we take and which company should we purchase them from? There are no simple answers other than to read and keep ourselves informed so that we can make wise choices. There are a number of excellent products that are on the market and researchers are improving on them every day. For the consumer this is good news if you are informed, but confusing if you don't know what you are being asked to buy.

Because the synergy of the natural properties of any supplement are likely to be altered in the manufacturing process, it is extremely important for us to be aware of the processes which are used in producing any supplement. We want to use supplements that are as close to their natural and unaltered state as is possible, in order to maximize effectiveness and minimize any potential negative consequences. Of course, the best solution is to eat lots of fresh raw fruits and vegetables daily (five to nine servings), but this is not always possible. Some people just plain don't like vegetables and others aren't able to get fresh produce because of location and season.

I think that in the future foodaceutical and nutriceutical supplementation will be a part of all of our daily routines. We have been taking vitamins and minerals for decades because we were taught that they were good for us. We were also taught by our mothers to eat our vegetables, although we didn't understand that eating them raw would be better for our health than eating them cooked.

The quality supplements that are available today combine the nutritional power of fruits and vegetables that naturally contain vitamins with digestive enzymes, phytochemicals and antioxidants to give us an easy to use option for our health. This contrasts with the vitamin and mineral supplements we have been taking over the last half-century. To put this in perspective, certain natural quality supplemental products available today are what colour television was to black and white TV. Particularly when they are compared to the vitamin and mineral supplements we have been taking for years. These quality supplements are improving almost daily in their effectiveness, and in their ability to improve and maintain our immune systems.

Addictions

"Every form of addiction is bad, no matter whether the narcotic be alcohol
or morphine or idealism."

—Carl Jung

Addictive substances are often the underlying cause, either directly or
indirectly, of virtually every illness, disease or trauma. And certainly
they are responsible for a majority of hospitalizations and doctors' visits.
To illustrate my point, I refer to the results of a study that was released in
June 1996 by the Canadian Centre on Substance Abuse located in Ottawa,
Canada.

National Findings:

> Substance abuse (which includes tobacco, alcohol and illicit
> drugs) cost Canadian society $18.45 billion in 1992 or $649
> per person.

Substance abuse-related deaths represented twenty-one per cent of
deaths from all causes in Canada in 1992. Potential years of life lost consti-
tuted twenty-three per cent of total years of life lost due to any cause.

When society combines these disturbing figures with productivity
losses from illness and premature death, the implications for the health
care system and the cost in human and financial terms are staggering. The
US, with ten times the population of Canada, would both mirror and
magnify these distressing numbers.

According to the readings I have done, most illness and disease can be traced back to nutrition and diet, which in turn will affect our psychological, emotional and physical health. The addictive substances that I am referring to are nicotine, alcohol, caffeine, sugar, illicit and over-the-counter drugs. Lifestyle can also lead to addictions like gambling.

You may ask the question, "What about hereditary factors?" Most hereditary factors are passed along through our DNA. The results of these hereditary factors are in all probability a reflection of what went on in our ancestors' lives through their living habits. This would account for factors that are sometimes inexplicable and that may appear to be inherited.

NICOTINE

Smoking is known beyond a doubt to be a major factor in the cause of many illnesses and disease, particularly cancer and heart disease. The negative implications of smoking can also be demonstrated through other not so obvious ways, as mentioned in the 21 October 1996 issue of *Time* magazine. In that particular issue, a research study was referenced that said that a pack or more a day of cigarettes can double a smoker's odds of developing macular degeneration, a disease of the retina that can lead to blindness. This is because smoking depletes the body of vital nutrients that may protect eyes from the disease.

In November 1996, the Ontario Medical Association issued a report that suggested that parents who smoke in homes with young children are practising child abuse. According to the OMA report: "Parental tobacco use in the home, resulting in the inhalation of known carcinogens and asthmagens by children, is a form of physical abuse."

Nicotine is the main substance that does the damage. Of course, like anything else, the degree to which a person indulges in the habit of smoking will affect any manifestation of disease. The effect on a person's overall health will also be as a result of other complementary lifestyle factors, such as activity level, dietary habits and stress levels.

In the context of health, it is simply not possible to be healthy and to smoke at the same time. The reason I say this is because the moment a person inhales from a cigarette there is an immediate negative effect on the body and respiratory system, beginning with the exchange of oxygen. The two, smoking and good health, are absolutely incongruent with each other and therefore are in contradiction.

I lived in the acute respiratory care unit of the University of Alberta Hospital for most of my life, and during that time virtually every respiratory ailment known to the medical profession was dealt with on our ward. This included illnesses and disease such as emphysema, lung cancer, bronchitis, asthma and certain other respiratory tract conditions that were either caused or exacerbated by smoking.

It was sad to see that so many people had their lives and those of their families ruined because of nicotine. This is to say nothing of the financial costs and sacrifices that both the individuals involved and their families would likely have endured over a lifetime. I distinctly remember people gasping for air and still using several litres of oxygen, yet hiding away in some corner (like a stairwell) or going outside in the freezing weather to have a puff on a cigarette, which had become such a ruling force in their lives.

I don't mean to sound judgmental, but often these people who found themselves in this predicament were not informed or aware of the dangers early enough in their life to realize what they were doing to themselves. Their condition had likely been manifested over a lifetime and now they were powerless to change their situation. If you talked to them about how they got started on this habit, it was often because their parents had done it or because of peer pressure at school.

I mentioned the cost to the individual and their families, but this is to say nothing of the financial crisis that virtually every health care system in the world finds itself in. Smoking, and thus nicotine, is a major factor that we must deal with if we are serious about our individual and collective health. There have certainly been attempts through No Smoking bylaws and increased taxes (that have sometimes been reversed, in Canada for example) to limit and control the incidence of smoking. Even though more people are quitting, there is almost an epidemic of smoking by teenagers and particularly among young women.

I think most adults who have decided to quit have done so for logical reasons, and often because of their children. When children find out that this is not good for you, the question becomes, "Why are you smoking, Mommy/Daddy?" This question can be a catalyst for some people.

I am reminded of a time when Valerie and I had taken our two children to a local mom and dad pizza shop that was contained in one room. We had picked out a table behind a lady and gentleman, where my four-year-old son Jamie had staked a claim. The gentleman lit up and smoke began to permeate the whole room. At this point, my son went up to him and said, "Hey, Mister, why are you smoking? " He did it in a very polite fashion and you could see the fellow begin to get uncomfortable with the question, even though he kind of smiled. Jamie then asked him, "Who taught you how to smoke?" He didn't respond to either question and at that point he got up, put his jacket on, and he and his lady friend left. Somehow I think there is a larger message for all of us in Jamie's question.

ALCOHOL

Alcohol is our most socially acceptable intoxicant and is used by virtually all societies. It has been used over the centuries for medicinal purposes and for the personal pleasure that it can sometimes provide. Alcohol, like most substances, can be useful and enjoyable when used intelligently and in moderation. Unfortunately, it can be like a car that is driven at excess speeds; in other words, dangerous. This is the way a great number of individuals use alcohol, to the detriment of themselves and others.

Alcohol has been linked to many of society's ills in the form of marriage breakdown, physical and mental abuse, financial ruin and crime. It has caused, either directly or indirectly, a great many health challenges both individually and collectively. Because it can be a highly addictive intoxicant, the problems that arise from the overuse of alcohol are often very difficult to correct. A major concern as we move into the twenty-first century is health care and its affordability. Alcohol is directly linked to affordability of the health care system.

Moderation again is the key when consuming alcohol. In small quantities it can have a calming effect and may even provide medicinal benefits. If taken to excess, it will become problematic. Excess is different for each person because of our biochemistry, weight, diet and, in general, the effects of our lifestyle on our bodily system.

Research into alcohol abuse shows that alcohol has many immediate and short-term effects on our system. For example, alcohol slows down the nervous system and can act as a depressant. Also, it consistently slows down the function of the brain and nervous system, and yet the early effects of ingesting alcohol are often increased activity and decreased inhibition. This apparent stimulating effect of alcohol actually results in depression from the inhibitory and behavioural control centres of the brain.

Alcohol has been linked with liver disease due mainly to the accumulation of fat in the liver cells. Normally this process is reversible, but with excess alcohol consumption it is too much for the liver to handle.

The adverse physical and psychological effects of long-term alcohol abuse can be debilitating or even fatal. They can result from the direct toxic effects of alcohol, or be secondary to nutritional deficiencies, use of other drugs and other lifestyle factors. Heavy alcohol use is a major cause of preventable brain deterioration and injury. It is interesting to note that as many as fifty to seventy per cent of detoxified alcoholics demonstrate some impairment on neuro-psychological testing of brain functions such as memory, perception and problem-solving capacity.

Chronic alcohol abuse is the single most prevalent cause of illness and death from liver disease, and liver disease itself is a leading cause of death. The liver is a metabolically complex organ and, therefore, is extremely important because it aids in the digestion of fats, sugars and the processing of proteins, and plays a significant role in blood circulation. Another liver function that is essential to our health is detoxification. It does this through the elimination of toxic chemicals, drugs and waste from our bodily system. A review of the medical effects of excess alcohol use reveals that almost all organs and systems of the body can be significantly affected. There is no question abuse of alcohol is a major cause of medical problems that often result in disability and/or death. The message is clear in that we need to be reasonable with alcohol consumption and, if we drink, we must do so in moderation.

Alcohol has probably impacted most of us in one way or another. In my life it provided me with an entertainment value when I was younger and more foolish than I am now and, conversely, it has robbed me of some very good friends and friendships. To illustrate what I mean, I used to travel extensively when I was involved as the executive director, and following that, as the president of the Canadian Wheelchair Sports Association. In order to travel and fulfil my voluntary duties, I needed the assistance of a willing and able friend or volunteer. This is because I am physically dependent on others for a great deal of my daily physical needs, such as transferring from my wheelchair to an airplane seat, into a bed, eating and generally just to get around. In order to do this I needed someone who I could rely on, and when alcohol became a factor with at least two of my travelling friends, I was no longer able to count on their reliability when travelling. This meant that I needed to cultivate additional friendships and willing volunteers who were more reliable than reliant on alcohol!

The other factor that was important in my case was that I use and rely on a respirator to breathe for me when I sleep at night. If there were any problems that would arise, such as the hoses accidentally becoming disconnected from the respirator, I needed the help of someone who could be counted on and was not intoxicated.

The other problem that complicates addressing alcohol excess is that the person who drinks to excess will often deny that there is a problem. If they don't recognize that there is a problem then it becomes very difficult to discuss their alcohol usage with them. This is because they become very defensive and then they deny your observations. At least this has been my experience. Needless to say, even though I had many good times with these friends and they were both kind and generous towards me, I had to let them know that I couldn't travel with them and be comfortable or confident in them when they were drinking. Eventually our friendships began to dissipate and I must take some of the responsibility for this.

My roommates and I were always trying new things and attempting new ventures with the intent of making money. We never did make much money, but we sure learned a lot through our many and varied experiences. One of our most credible ventures was when we got into the computer software business way back in 1970. We may have been a little ahead of our time in that we were in the right business, but we were a little short on experience and the company was under-capitalized. The company was called Pro-Data Services Ltd. and we specialized in custom software systems. We started Pro-Data in the University Hospital and, after experiencing some growth, we moved into an apartment across the street. After a couple of years in this apartment we expanded and required the more businesslike environment that was usually consistent with being in a regular office complex. Moving from the institutional environment provided by the University Hospital and progressing to an office complex in the downtown core was akin to a country bumpkin moving to the big city! When we started this company there were six of us involved and we all took on complementary roles. This leads me into the next example of how alcohol abuse affected me personally.

In this case, one of my ex-roommates, who was also one of my business partners, was under significant personal and business pressure. To relieve the stress he would often have a shot of scotch when he got home from work. After doing this for two or three years he eventually progressed to several shots of scotch on a regular basis. The office of Pro-Data Services Ltd. was located in an office downtown, and next door there was a pub that he began to frequent. On this particular day he left the office a little early to imbibe in the manner to which he had become accustomed and he became rather inebriated in short order. On top of his intoxicated condition he also had some breathing impairments and, like me, he used a respirator to sleep with at night. On this particular day, he was met as usual by the disabled transportation driver who worked for the city, but in this case he passed out on the way home from work in the back of the Disabled Adult Transportation van which was transporting him back to the Aberhart Centre.

For people who can breathe normally this would be no big deal, but in this case my friend didn't get enough air and became deficient in oxygen consumption. By the time he got back to the Aberhart facility he was already a ghastly colour, even though the van ride only took about fifteen minutes. Ten days later he died in intensive care due to the brain damage that he suffered when he lost control after passing out. All of this was preventable and only happened because my good friend had become hooked on the bottle. We not only lost a friend and brother, but eventually we had to close the doors of our ten-year-old company, Pro-Data Services Ltd., because he was the business head and the driving force in our company. The impact of his dependency on alcohol had huge ramifications beyond his own demise, for his family, friends and business colleagues.

Most people in our North American society have been affected by the abuse of alcohol, either directly or indirectly. We have probably known someone, either personally or through friends, who has been involved in an alcohol-related accident. Every day it is in the news, so there is no escaping the impact that it has on society. One of the problems with alcohol abuse is that we collectively have come to accept it as commonplace and we may actually have become numbed and insensitive to its consequences. Maybe we can't always affect the use of alcohol by others, but we can be aware of how overuse of any substance, and especially alcohol, can impact our health. Armed with this understanding, we again should remember that moderation is the key.

CAFFEINE

The most common use of caffeine occurs when we drink coffee and tea. Normally, we don't tend to think of tea and coffee as addictive substances, but they can be and it is the caffeine to which we become addicted. Caffeine also is contained in a number of other beverages and foodstuffs, such as many popular soft drinks and a variety of sweets containing chocolate. Most of these products are enjoyed by consumers everywhere. When they are taken in small amounts they often have a short-term pleasurable effect and, on occasion, a useful therapeutic benefit. However, for the most part we North Americans over-consume substantial amounts of coffee, tea, pop and chocolates on an annual basis.

The chairperson of the University of Alberta's Department of Agriculture, Food and Nutritional Science thinks it's time that the issue of caffeine and health be opened to public debate. He says, "Caffeine is the only drug that is widely added to the food supply. It is an addictive stimulant and scientific research has demonstrated that caffeine consumption affects reproduction, behaviour and bone mineral metabolism, and has negative nutritional consequences for children."

I remember the first time I ever heard of caffeine poisoning and how impossible that seemed to me at the time. The term was used to describe a condition of one of my mother's close friends. It turns out that this woman consumed approximately thirty cups of coffee on a daily basis. She was being treated for an apparent neurological or psychological disorder that was precipitated by excess caffeine consumption. I then began to understand the consequences of drinking excess amounts of any beverage, let alone coffee.

When I was in my late teens and early twenties I used to experience heart palpitations or the occasional skipping of a heartbeat. This was disconcerting, mainly because when I first got polio I was treated with a heart medication called digitalis. Evidently this was necessitated because my heart had stopped, likely as a result of cardiopulmonary difficulties. All I know was that I had missed about thirty-six hours while I was unconscious and that my right hand was swollen when I regained consciousness. As I recall, I had a big needle mark in the back of my hand. I was told that this is where they injected a drug to get my heart going properly again.

When I became a teenager I fancied myself as being an adult and started doing more adult things. Drinking coffee was something that I enjoyed doing even if I wasn't sure why! It certainly couldn't have been the taste because the University Hospital coffee was for the most part too strong, too bitter and was of questionable taste. Every week the volunteers would come and help us with various activities and often these kind-hearted women would make a freshly brewed urn of coffee for the residents. In the beginning I was excluded by my age. On occasion, however, I was able to talk them into giving me a cup or two and, boy, did it taste good. Drinking coffee was one of the very enjoyable activities that we took part in, simply because of the social aspect that came along with it.

When I started experiencing palpitations and other heart irregularities I became concerned and was tested for all kinds of things. It was recommended that I should either eliminate coffee altogether or, at the very least, limit consumption to one or two cups per day. It was also recommended that I not drink Coca-Cola because of the caffeine content. I drank very little pop anyway, so this was not a problem for me. But coffee was another story because I drank several cups a day. I was also told that the irregularities I was experiencing were not life threatening. Because of this, although I was aware of my coffee consumption and tried to control it, I didn't quit drinking coffee or tea until I turned forty-six.

At this age I experienced some significant pain and discomfort resulting from an esophageal reflex problem which was exacerbated when I drank tea or coffee. The pain was scary in that it was very intense and made me wonder if I was experiencing a heart attack. Fortunately, it wasn't a heart attack and it was what I needed to make me decide to quit drinking caffeinated beverages. I must admit that I feel significantly better now that I have stopped and not only that, I am much healthier for having made the decision to quit. The esophageal reflex problem hasn't returned since then. Lately, more and more of my friends are giving up coffee for health-related reasons and find that once they get past the initial withdrawal stages they also feel much better for having done so.

SUGAR

We think of sugar as something that we enjoy and often view it as a treat in the form of dessert or candy. We don't view it as an addictive substance or as something that is detrimental to society as a whole. I guarantee that if you read a book entitled *Sugar Blues*, authored by William Dufty and published by Warner Books, you will no doubt take another look at the effect the refining of sugar has had, and is having, on our populations.

I won't go into details about what is contained in the book; however, I would urge you to investigate the subject of sugar and its larger effect on our society. The reason I suggest this is that we all know an excess of sugar in our diets cannot be healthy for us, but most of us don't have a clue as to why. We think that most things if taken in moderation will be okay and our body will be able to adjust accordingly. This is probably true in most cases, but when dealing with substances that are addictive in nature it is often very difficult to stop at moderation.

In my previous work as chairperson of the Alberta Premier's Council on the Status of Persons with Disabilities, I saw the end result in the form of disabling conditions that people need to deal with. There were many causes and effects, but the increase in incidence of certain conditions is at times almost incomprehensible. The cost in human and financial terms is ever mounting and our collective response is to take several approaches, but very seldom do we attempt to look at the root cause. A specific example is diabetes and the many and varied consequences of this disease. Our response is to solicit public funds and to pour money into research, which has resulted in small and mostly insignificant gains. We always tend to look for the magic cure rather than facing the culprit squarely in the eye. There is no question that the worldwide increase in sugar consumption, particularly in modern societies, has caused significant increases in diseases such as diabetes. Not only that, but the incidence of blindness, circulatory difficulties and amputation brings with it a whole new set of costs and challenges.

It is very difficult to get away from sugar as it is presented to us in a variety of very popular products. Our consumption of these products is the result of being force-fed a steady diet of advertising both overt and subliminal, in the name of profit, which at times can be contradictory to our health. It is this kind of aggressive corporate action that has an effect on our lives and sometimes that effect can be negative.

The point is that we, both collectively and individually, are influenced and manipulated without realizing it. This is sad because it affects us and the decisions that we make, as well as having potential generational influences that are passed down to our offspring. We do this through the environment we create for our children, the culture in which we bring them up and by passing on through our genetic code a whole host of influences that are a by-product of lifestyle.

Refining products such as sugar, wheat and rice has created a couple of dynamics that we should be aware of. First of all, it has led to a number of industries that have created economic spin-offs and benefits for various economies. It has generated huge profits, primarily for multi-national corporations and their shareholders worldwide. At the same time, refined products have created a dependency in the population, with the biggest dependency being created by our addiction to the sugars that are added to a large number of products. Our individual daily consumption of sugar has gone through the roof, and with it has come a multiplicity of serious challenges in the form of illness, disease, various disabilities and other inexplicable behavioural disorders. Kevin Trudeau of Mega-Memory fame says that sugar impairs our ability to concentrate. If he is correct, is it possible that if the ability to concentrate is impaired, that it could then manifest itself as a perceived behavioural disorder? If so, think of the implications.

My personal experience has been with our son, who exhibits definite behavioural changes after having candies or other sweets. I am sure that in this day and age most teachers would think that he is an extremely bright child with a great deal of potential in most instances. If sugar is, or becomes a part of his regular diet, they will not be seeing this kid for his potential, but rather for his non-conforming behaviour. It is these behavioural challenges that teachers are left to deal with in a classroom, and that have put them in a position of looking for help. Most times this help is prescribed in the form of Ritalin or some other mood-altering drug. This in turn masks the real problem and in itself can create another life-long dependency, with who knows what consequences.

We are often left to deal with symptoms and situations that have an underlying cause of which we are not aware. In our society today we are used to looking for quick fixes and a magic cure in the form of medication. As a consequence, we have put an unbelievable amount of power and control in the hands of the pharmaceutical industry and the doctors who dispense drugs on their behalf.

The root cause of many illnesses and disease can be traced to so-called addictive substances and sugar, which appears relatively harmless, may actually be the worst of them all.

I have worked for many years in the field of removing barriers for people with disabilities. People have acquired their disability through a variety of circumstances and events during their lives, but ultimately they are left to deal with the multiplicity of complicating factors that arise as a result of their new condition in life. Conditions such as diabetes have many negative ramifications that come with a huge cost, both in financial and in human terms. Not only is the person who lives with the condition affected, so are their family, friends, employer and the community that they live in.

The human body is an amazing machine and in most instances has the capacity to filter out many undesired chemicals and other unwanted waste from our bodies. However, when we overdo it with any type of excess, our bodily system will rebel and attempt to cleanse itself in any number of ways. Often the cleansing will present itself through the manifestation of an illness, or a disease such as diabetes. At this stage it really is a drastic wake-up call and is a crucial signal for us to change our lifestyle. Unfortunately, it often has to come to a crisis before we get the message to treat our bodies with more respect. Our body can handle most things in moderation but all too often people don't stop there, particularly with addictive substances such as sugar. Remember, moderation, or sometimes abstinence, is the key.

PROBLEM GAMBLING

We don't tend to think of gambling in the same vein as other addictive behaviours. However, authorities who have extensively researched this subject have proven beyond a doubt that there can be dire health consequences. Governments everywhere are facilitating gambling opportunities and have become hooked on the gaming revenue that has proven so lucrative. They themselves are like junkies!

In its paper titled "The A, B, Cs of Problem Gambling," the Alberta Alcohol and Drug Abuse Commission (AADAC) talks about some of the negative impacts on our individual and collective health as a consequence of this addictive behaviour. Even though the study was done for AADAC, the research was extensive and far reaching, and probably is applicable to most modern societies.

The consequences of problem gambling affect many aspects of our lives including: personal, social, spiritual, emotional, physical, financial, professional and legal.

The physical consequences are often stress-related, e.g., loss of appetite and sleep, digestive problems, anxiety attacks, cardiac problems, high blood pressure, back or neck pain, diabetes and hypertension.

The effects for the family are often expressed through interpersonal conflict, alienation, lack of stability, family breakdown, separation or divorce, neglect, disregard for safety and an increased risk of problems for children.

Again, the message is clear: if we are going to partake, then moderation is the key.

My experiences with gambling were in my teens and in my twenties, when my roommates and I would bet on virtually everything that moved. I was introduced to horse racing when I was about thirteen and it got in my blood. We used to go to the racetrack almost every day and there didn't seem to be a shortage of willing volunteers to take us to the track. My first experience at the track was a winning experience and I made approximately twenty-eight dollars after winning the quinella on the final race of the day. From then on I was hooked on betting. None of us had very much money or regular income. As for me, I just saved and used my allowance.

In fact we were such enthusiasts that my roommates and I designed and developed a horse racing game called Pounding Hooves that we used to play by the hour. It was a lot of fun because any number of people could play it at one time. It was designed so that we could mimic and simulate most aspects of racing, including betting even though it was only for nickels and dimes. We thought that the game was so good, we naively tried to manufacture and market it ourselves.

My grandmother lived in England and used to correspond with me on a regular basis. When I told her about my interest in horse racing and betting she became very concerned because gambling was a problem for both her father and brother. I guess she was afraid that I was going to wind up in the same situation. Betting was almost a way of life for some people in the early 1900s, and still is a large influence in the British culture, with betting shops being very prevalent. She probably had good reason to be concerned, but fortunately for me I found other things to do with my time and my allowance.

DRUGS

Drugs come in different forms and some are legal while others are not, but we shouldn't be fooled by the fact that a particular drug may be legal. Fooled in the sense that because it is legal doesn't mean that it can't or won't be harmful to us. There are many instances where people have become innocent victims of dependency on over-the-counter drugs. Some people have become dependent on painkillers that are easily obtainable and meant for short-term use, however they can result in long term addiction or dependency. This is to say nothing about the epidemic use and dependency on prescription drugs that is occurring at an increasing and alarming rate in our modern-day society.

Legal drugs can be just as dangerous to our health as illegal drugs are known to be. In 1995, the *Canadian Medical Association Journal* published a study that found that the doctors who wrote the most prescriptions also had the highest death rates among their patients. This study found that some doctors, in trying to maximize the number of patients they could process per day, did not take the time necessary to find out what was wrong with these patients. That kind of medical practice results in over-medicated and inappropriately medicated patients. It increases the risk of adverse reactions, and it is costly.

Even though the controlled studies and pharmaceutical propaganda suggest that drugs such as Prozac and Ritalin are not dangerous or addictive, there is evidence from former users that extended usage did create problems of dependency for those individuals.

The use of prescription drugs under the guise of medicinal reasons is often a sign of our inability to handle situations that require either an emotional or social solution. In my previous work at the Premier's

Council I talked with and read about several individuals who were negatively affected with medications that were prescribed by well-meaning doctors. Medications can often hide emotional pain and sometimes they mask the corresponding symptoms, which must be dealt with in order to prevent future health challenges. We have been cultured to look for quick solutions and often find it easier to go to our doctor and get a prescription rather than deal with the real problem or issue. We then pass this mentality along to our children, which results in perpetuating and exacerbating the problems of dependency and addiction.

We must understand that if we avoid dealing with emotional issues today, they will then present themselves as health problems tomorrow. It can be compared to a balloon that is filled with air, in the sense that when you squeeze or poke it, it will bulge and reshape itself in other places through reconfiguration. This, too, will happen with our emotions in that they will manifest themselves in other ways that may be problematic for our health if we suppress or mask them through the misplaced use of medications. The simple message in all this is that we all too often look to a solution that is quick and easy by turning to our doctors for medications. The other irony in all this is that by initially looking for a quick fix, we may have created or begun the manifestation of problems that in the future may require antibiotic treatment.

ANTIBIOTICS

The problems that are now surfacing because of the overuse and inappropriate use of antibiotics have resulted in tremendous challenges for our immune systems. The reason is that many forms of bacteria have now become resistant to the antibiotics currently being used, antibiotics which were previously effective in combating these same bacterial infections. The interesting thing about bacteria that often results in bacterial infection is that this same bacteria is usually prevalent in our body at all times. What makes the bacterial infection problematic is that our immune system may have become weakened for any number of reasons, where before it may have been strong enough to have staved off the bacterial attack.

In my life antibiotics played a major role, as I was dependent on them for over forty years to help me combat respiratory infections. I also was on tetracycline for several years because of my acne problems. I now know that my acne was attributable to my dietary habits, whereas before I just thought it was because I was a teenager. I guess I should have clued in earlier, because I still had problems with acne well into my thirties! Because of overuse and some times inappropriate use of antibiotics, I have personally experienced antibiotic-resistant bacterial infections. This resulted in prolonged and changing antibiotic therapy. Each change brought with it the need for a stronger more targeted dosage, whereas before I could manage with a lower dose in the form of a less-targeted, broad-spectrum medication.

Maybe I wasn't addicted in the true sense, but I definitely had become dependent on drugs in the form of antibiotics.

I was reading a medical newsletter and the topic was the race against the evolution of bacteria by researchers in the field of antibiotics. In the article the author explained that in an ongoing act of self-preservation, bacteria are outsmarting researchers, physicians and pharmaceutical companies at an alarming rate. Therefore, it is no longer possible for physicians to prescribe an antibiotic with certainty that it will kill a bug because bacteria are now smart enough to dodge almost any drug that is thrown at them.

Bacteria have become shining examples of Darwin's credo, "survival of the fittest." The article continues with a further description of the challenges facing us in the future around the use of antibiotics and quotes one doctor as saying,

> There are only a number of ways we can beat antibiotic resistance: being careful with the drugs we have, trying to invent new drugs and improving sanitary conditions to stop the proliferation of bacteria.

The author speculates that bacteria are clever enough that they can figure out a way around everything we design, and he thinks that we're unlikely to ever find that "something" that's magic. He believes that the answer lies in not trying to defeat bacteria, but in keeping one step ahead of them.

I think it is interesting to note that the doctor who was quoted talked about some of the things that may be able to be done to combat antibiotic resistance. It is also interesting to consider the things that he didn't mention, such as keeping the immune system strong through good nutrition, a healthy lifestyle and exercise. I speculate that he didn't mention these things because of the medical mindset that accompanies his professional training. I suggest, however, that his comments are to be taken very seriously by all of us, and really they are a strong warning for us to take care of our bodies and to keep our immune systems strong and healthy. If we don't take care of ourselves it appears that we won't be able to rely on medications the way we have for the past couple of decades, even if we find ourselves in a medical crisis.

To give you more of an idea of some of the challenges surrounding antibiotic use, the 1995 annual report of the Patented Medicine Prices Review Board of Canada revealed that Canadians consumed fifteen per cent more drugs in 1995 than the year before. In the same period, the average price of patent medicines fell 1.75 per cent but total spending rose ten per cent. The annual report continued to say that the increased consumption seemed to be larger than could be accounted for by the aging of the population. The chairman of the Review Board was quoted as saying that he could "only presume that the increase may be caused by over-prescribing."

Fortunately for me, I have learned a great deal about my health, about medicine and medications, about healthy lifestyles and about how to better take care of my whole person. This has had tremendous positive implications for my health because I have virtually eliminated the need for regular antibiotic treatments for respiratory infections. The reason I have been able to eliminate antibiotic treatments is for the most part because I am now healthier and am now better able to handle, through natural immunological responses, the bacteria that previously presented problems in the form of infections. This has resulted in an improved quality of life for me, and my family. Thanks be to the many tough and hard lessons that resulted in my education and enlightenment!

Conclusion

Many people describe being healthy as the absence of illness and disease. We can have the absence of the symptoms of illness and disease but still be unhealthy, with illness lurking in the background like a bobcat waiting for its prey. I prefer to think of being healthy as having the energy and stamina to do what I want, when I want, with whomever I want. In most cases, when a person is experiencing the onset of health problems, his or her energy level is often the first thing to be affected.

Most of us live in fear of acquiring a life-altering illness or disease and few of us ever see it as an opportunity to address past unresolved issues in our lives. There is a plethora of information and a myriad of personal stories that chronicle and document that when illness or disease presents itself, the opportunity is also there to do some real healing. This healing usually touches the deepest part of our being, and that is our soul. The odds are that it will be extremely difficult for the individual who is afflicted with an illness or disease and their family, to see the silver lining amidst the dark cloud of illness.

What makes it extremely difficult, in addition to the trauma of the situation, is our personal and societal preoccupation with the physical aspect of our lives. However, in all likelihood, if they can see the opportunity for healing beyond the physical, they will be healthier and better off than before they were presented with what was originally thought to be an unfortunate situation.

On many occasions, I have seen where an individual and his family were forced to deal with what was thought to be a personal tragedy but turned out to be a time for them to confront the past. A past that had been an anticipated fearful experience, and one which was to be avoided.

This brings up the point about the avoidance of many things in our lives. Avoidance is commonly expressed through denial and, figuratively speaking, running from our true feelings and emotions. These feelings and emotions may be in the form of suppressed anger, frustration or sexual anxieties and relate to earlier experiences in our lives and, therefore, may be difficult for us to pinpoint.

It is never too late to acknowledge these negative feelings and emotions, whether they involve others or not. Most of all though, we need to forgive ourselves as part of the healing process. The healing of most illnesses and diseases won't happen until we address the underlying causes. It is worth noting that anytime an illness or disease presents itself, it usually has a cause behind it in the form of some unresolved issue or happening from earlier in life. Becoming ill and recognizing the perhaps hidden source of our ailment can be an opportunity for personal growth. If we seize this opportunity we will heal and not only that, our circle of influence, in the form of family, friends and associates, will also feel the benefits of our personal healing.

A SIMPLE TOOL—"FAITH"

Earlier on, I gave you the "WISER" method as a simple and easy-to-remember tool to improve your physical health. As a companion piece to the WISER way, I offer a reminder that faith can be an emotional, psychological and spiritual tool. Health and personal well-being are dependent on the spirit as well as the body.

There are five elements to what I call the "FAITH" tool and these elements are summarized as:

1. "F" stands for forgiveness of yourself and others.
2. "A" stands for acceptance of people and situations.
3. "I" stands for integrity in all aspects of our lives.
4. "T" stands for trust in our fellow man and ourselves.
5. "H" stands for honesty, humility and humour.

When you combine the WISER and FAITH tools in your daily life, you will have a simple yet powerful ally in your quest for a healthier life.

A FINAL THOUGHT

The next century promises great advancements in the area of biotechnology. These advancements will have significant impacts in medical care and on our daily lives. We are already experiencing the influence of genetic engineering, particularly in the agricultural sector. This influence reaches our table every day, through the many different foods that we purchase at our corner grocery store. Unless we are diligent readers of labels, most of us are totally unaware of what we are ingesting in the way of genetically altered foods.

The human genome project, which is a collaboration of efforts on the part of certain governments, governmental agencies and industry, will give mankind an understanding of the genetic makeup of the human body like never before. The results of this new understanding for society will be a double-edged sword. It will lead to designer drugs or antibiotics for virtually anything that we consider problematic for the human condition. It will also present us with ethical challenges that were unimaginable just a few short years ago.

This new information may be overpowering for most people, making it difficult for us to know which, or what, is the best thing to do in any given situation involving our personal health. Therefore, it is important to remember that we have the right, the responsibility and the personal power, to affect our health. The reason it is important to remember this is because it is the only thing that we can rely on.

We have many God-given tools that are at our disposal, and I have tried to capture some of them as they have been gleaned through my personal experiences. What I have attempted to do in writing this book is to give people both the information and reasons why each and every one of us must take responsibility for our individual and collective health. Also, I have tried to differentiate between what health really is, and that which we currently call health care, and what in my experience is really a medical care system disguised as a health care system. We have been both deceived and mistaken by using this terminology to describe the illness and disease model that is so much a part of our everyday lives.

I believe we must work to design a system of health that will support healthy lifestyles rather than perpetuate the illness and disease framework that we currently have. A good place to start would be to use different labels when describing that which is truly medical care and crisis driven, versus health and wellness. Also, we must acknowledge and realize that it is virtually impossible to create this system of health through the illness and disease culture that is perpetuated by our post-secondary education system. A culture that is further perpetuated by those with profit-driven and powerful self-interests. We must regain personal control of our health and societal wellness by doing all we can to create healthy lifestyles. Hopefully, you have found my attempt at sharing both informative and useful.

When we are not well, or are in pain, we know, feel and experience this personal discomfort. Conversely, when we feel well, we often take it for granted, forgetting that our thoughts, words and subsequent actions, both internally and externally, affect our health and often those around us. Simply by being more aware and by using our common sense, we can significantly impact our collective health through simple daily actions.

The old saying, "An apple a day..." is as true now as it was then and can serve as our daily reminder, "that if it's going to be, it's up to me." Together, we can change the culture by personally demonstrating that health care is not medical care, and that true health care comes through self-care.

In closing I want to leave you with this thought. When we are done on this earth with life, as we currently know it, it is what we leave behind in the form of intangibles that is really important. It doesn't matter how many material things we leave behind, or how much money we will to others. It does matter, however, whether we leave behind unresolved issues, particularly if others are involved. I guess this begs the question, "Why do we often wait for tragedy to enter our lives before we address what is really important?" We should always remember the words of Harriet Beecher Stowe:

> The bitterest tears shed over graves are for words left unsaid and deeds left undone.

Appendix

RECOMMENDED READING

Attwood, Charles, *Dr. Attwood's Low-Fat Prescription for Kids*, Penguin Books, 375 Hudson Street, New York NY 10014.

Bateson-Koch, Carolee, *Allergies–Disease in Disguise*, Alive Books, 7436 Fraser Park Drive, Burnaby BC V5J 5B9.

Batmanghelidj, F., *Your Body's Many Cries for Water*, Global Health Solutions Inc., PO Box 3189, Falls Church VA 22043.

Burton Goldberg Group, *Alternative Medicine–The Definitive Guide*, Future Medicine Publishing Inc., 5009 Pacific Hwy. E, Suite 6 Fife, Washington 98424.

Chopra, Deepak, *Perfect Health, The Complete Mind/Body Guide*, Harmony Books, 201 East 50th Street, New York NY 10022.

Dossey, Larry, *Healing Words*, HarperCollins Publishers, 10 East 53rd Street, New York NY 10022.

Dufty, William, *Sugar Blues*, Warner Books, PO Box 690, New York NY 10019.

Durst, Michael, *Napkin Notes On the Art of Living*, Centre for the Art of Living, PO Box 788, Evanston, Illinois 60204.

Egoscue, Pete, *The Egoscue Method of Health Through Motion*, HarperCollins Publishers, 10 East 53rd Street, New York NY 10022.

Mendelsohn, Robert S., *How to Raise a Healthy Child...In Spite of Your Doctor*, Ballantine Books, New York NY.

Moore, Thomas, *Care of the Soul*, HarperCollins Publishers Inc., 10 East 53 St., New York NY 10022.

Regehr Clark, Hulda, *The Cure for All Diseases*, New Century Press, 2232 Verus Street, Suite D, San Diego CA 92154.

Santillo, Humbart "Smokey," *Intuitive Eating*, Hohm Press, PO Box 2501, Prescott AZ 86302.

Tice, Lou, *Smart Talk for Achieving Your Potential*, Pacific Institute Publishing, Waterfront Place 800, 1011 Western Ave., Seattle WA 98104.